STORIES THAT ASTONISH

The Parables of Jesus

Prentice Meador

Stories that Astonish: The Parables of Jesus

HillCrest
PUBLISHING

1648 Campus Court
Abilene, TX 79601

Cover design by Angie Maddox.

Typesetting by Tigris Creative Studios, LLC, Fort Worth, Texas.
www.tigrisstudios.com

Printed in the United States of America

ISBN 0-89112-446-2

Library of Congress Card Number **00-105861**

1,2,3,4,5

To My Heroes

Prentice A. Meador, Sr.
Bill Staggs
Byron Nelson
John Wooden
Batsell B. Baxter

For these men I have the deepest
appreciation and admiration.

Acknowledgements

A whole bunch of people have encouraged, urged, and beaten up on me to get this book done.

Special thanks to:

Charme Robarts and Thom Lemmons, my editors. You both knew what my manuscript needed. Thanks for making valuable suggestions and urging me to complete the task. It's been fun working with you.

Dave Malone, my associate. Thanks for writing the material for discussion and small groups. Lots of people will be in your debt. I am, too.

Malinda Gowan, my secretary. Thank you so much for typing the entire manuscript. You do much more than type; your encouragement helped me get the book done.

Barbara Meador, my dear wife. Thanks for laughing at my stories and always being there for me. You are my deepest love.

This book had its beginning in the summer of 1975 at Vanderbilt University Divinity Library, where I began work on a series of sermons on the parables of Christ. That series was later published as *Who Rules Your Life.*

I bear complete responsibility for the weaknesses in this book. Had it not been for those listed above, there would have been more of them.

TABLE OF CONTENTS

1

LET ME TELL
YOU A STORY

Seems like I've always loved stories. When
Mom would put me to bed as a child, she would
take down the Hurlbut's Bible Story Book and
read one to me. I loved to hear the one about
David and Goliath. Couldn't turn out the light
and go to sleep without a story. Cars run on gas.
Our family runs on stories. Between Dad and my
uncle Bill, we were constantly treated to stories,
usually funny, usually at mealtime. Like the one
that happened when they were young and seining
Short's Creek for fish. (It was against Tennessee
law to seine.) As they pulled out the seine net,
there was a large bass hung in the net. As they
were about to keep it, they heard a deep voice up
above them on the bank say, "Throw him back."
Thinking it was a game warden, they did.
Quickly! Then they looked up to see that the
voice came from a young man who was about 12
years old. His voice was changing and he fooled
them. For years after that moment, whenever any
one of us caught a nice size fish, someone would
always say in a deep voice, "Throw him back."

During special family meals, Dad would

gather us around the table and after a great feast of country ham, he would launch one of his stories. He took extraordinary pains to describe every hair on a shaggy dog, every bend in a crooked road. We would plead with him to "hurry up," but to his great delight, he would string the story out till we were all exhausted. Even if we had heard his stories a hundred times, we all laughed, thinking just maybe he wouldn't tell them again. But he did. And we loved them.

God loves stories too! That's the way he chose to communicate. Wonder why? As the Creator of the universe and having all available power, why does he tell us stories? Maybe because we all love stories. Stories make children of us all. Maybe because we remember stories. We forget dry facts, but when someone says, "Let me tell you a story," all ears tune in. Maybe because he wants us to get the point. We participate in his stories. As we listen to them, we say things like, "That's me." "I feel that way." "I've done that too."

Whatever his reasons, God opens his heart to us in stories. They're called "parables."

A Definition

When I was a child growing up in middle Tennessee, I heard a "parable" defined as "an earthly story with a heavenly meaning." I don't know who came up with that definition, but it's not a bad one. For heaven and earth do meet in the parables of Jesus.

Later I learned that a parable is a particular type of metaphor or simile. It's a word-picture. Like all figures of speech, it "implies an intuitive perception of a similarity in dissimilars."[1] It is, as one writer says, "drawn from nature or common life"; and its power lies in its ability to arrest the hearer by its vividness or strangeness, leaving the mind in sufficient doubt about its precise application to tease it into active thought."[2] A parable then, is a point of comparison between an accepted truth in the reality of the natural world and a new, similar truth in the reality of the spiritual world.

"The Hebrew [for] parable, *mashal*, has a wide range of meanings," Brad Young reminds us. "It may refer to a proverb, riddle, anecdote, fable, or allegory.... The *mashal* begins where the listener is, but then pushes beyond the new realm of discovery."[3] Jesus creates connections between events that are obvious in the natural world and the equally basic truths of the spiritual realm—how daily life intersects eternal truth. It's a powerful form, as Fred Craddock reminds us: it "...draws the listener into personal involvement, and leaves the final resolution of the issue to the hearer's own judgment."[4] As Jesus offers the rule

---

1   Aristotle, *Poetics*, 1449a.

2   C.H. Dodd, *The Parables of the Kingdom*, (New York: Scribner's, 1961), 16.

3   Brad H. Young, *The Parables* (Peabody, Mass.: Hendrickson Publishers, Inc., 1998), 3.

4   Fred Craddock, *Overhearing the Gospel* (Nashville: Abington Press, 1978), 77.

of God to us, he lifts us from the routine, humdrum, and dull thud of the daily grind to a higher plane of abundant living. He uses his parables as vehicles to accomplish his goal. It works, too!

The parables make up more than one-third of Jesus' recorded teaching.[5] They are also perennially popular. The stories of the Good Samaritan and The Prodigal Son are among the best-loved stories of both children and adults. Jesus carefully weaves his parables out of every day life. And in his hands, the parable becomes a powerful instrument—compelling our closest attention.

Building Blocks of a Parable

1. Prologue. Often Jesus introduces one of his stories with, "The kingdom of heaven is like...." The prologue gains the audience's attention and prepares them for the forthcoming story.

2. Characters. Jesus then presents his cast of characters. He might say, for example, "A man was going down from Jerusalem to Jericho, when he fell into the hands of robbers. They stripped him of his clothes, beat him and went away, leaving him half dead." Each character is vital to his story.

3. Storyline. Jesus unfolds his plot, as when the Samaritan stops to aid the dying man

---

5 A.M. Hunter, *Interpreting The Parables* (Philadelphia: The Westminster Press, 1960), 7

after a priest and Levite failed to stop and help. The story line may center in a paradox, a conflict, an ambiguity.

4. Point. Jesus will insist on us facing the paradox, solving the conflict,   clearing the ambiguity. "Which of these three do you think was a neighbor to the man who fell into the hands of robbers?" Jesus wants us, of course, to apply the spiritual point. It's the take-home.

List of Parables

The particular list of parables is based upon several measures. First, most scholars recognize these parables as full and complete, not mere figures of speech or epigrams of Jesus. Second, all these parables focus upon the kingdom, its proclamation and explanation. By this distinctive figure, the parable, Jesus conferred power and prominence upon the kingdom. Third, all these parables are found in Matthew, Mark, and Luke. (Not included are the figurative sayings of Jesus such as the "I am ..." statements recorded in John.)

All Bible references are from the New International Version, unless otherwise indicated.

Each chapter includes an explanation of the cultural references in each parable to first-century Palestinian life and the world in which Jesus lives. I've retold each story in bold type. Obviously, no one can retell the parables better than Jesus tells them. By interpreting the stories of Jesus, I make an attempt to paraphrase, restate, and seek the

List of Parables

The Wise and Foolish Builders	Matthew 7:24-29
New Garment, New Wine Skin	Matthew 9:16-17; Mark 2:21-22; Luke 5:36-38
Sower	Matthew 13:3-8; Mark 4:3-8; Luke 8:5-8
Weeds	Matthew 13:24-30; 36-43
Mustard Seed and Yeast	Matthew 13:31-35; Mark 4:30-34; Luke 13:18-21
Hidden Treasure and Pearl	Matthew 13:44-46
Net	Matthew 13:47-52
Lost Sheep	Matthew 18:10-14; Luke 15:1-7
Unmerciful Servant	Matthew 18:21-35
Workers in the Vineyard	Matthew 20:1-16
Two Sons	Matthew 21:28-32
Tenants	Matthew 21:33-46; Mark 12:1-12; Luke 20:9-19
Wedding Banquet	Matthew 22:1-14
The Budding Fig Tree	Matthew 24:32-35; Mark 13:28-32
The Ten Virgins	Matthew 25:1-13
Talents	Matthew 25:14-30
Growing Seed	Mark 4:26-29
Two Debtors	Luke 7:36-50
Good Samaritan	Luke 10:25-37
The Persistent Host	Luke 11:5-10
The Unclean Spirit	Luke 11:24-26
Rich Fool	Luke 12:16-21
Steward with Supervision	Luke 12:42-46
The Barren Fig Tree	Luke 13:6-9
Great Banquet	Luke 14:15-24
The Tower Builder and King at War	Luke 14:28-32
Lost Coin	Luke 15:8-10
Lost Son	Luke 15:11-32
Shrewd Manager	Luke 16:1-18
The Rich Man and Lazarus	Luke 16:19-31
Persistent Widow	Luke 18:1-8
Pharisee and Tax Collector	Luke 18:9-14
Ten Minas	Luke 19:11-27

hidden meaning that Jesus intends. In the final section of each chapter, we'll look for modern applications to our own lives. Questions for discussion conclude each chapter.

Why Do These Stories Astonish Us?

Why are the parables of Jesus so powerful and popular? Several characteristics of his parables offer clues.

1. The parables of Jesus are oral. As Jesus tells each parable, it comes across with great power. This seems to be true partly because the parables are oral, not written down and passed out to the audience. There is something about them that grabs your attention when he says, "Let me tell you a story." But not everybody can tell a good story.

Certain traits are common to any good story and the parables of Jesus are no exception. An effective story is conversational in tone. A parable is informal, directed to real people, and lends itself to ordinary conversation. Jesus tells many of his parables in the context of other conversations around a table, in the streets, and in the ordinary places of daily living.

> *There is something about them that grabs your attention when he says, "Let me tell you a story." But not everybody can tell a good story.*

Another trait of a good story is its ability to hold your interest and attention. You can identify with the point of the story. No wonder the Bible records no instance of his audience going to sleep or of anyone walking out. How could a person walk away from a good story?

2. The parables of Jesus have a single message. "Taken altogether," writes Bruce Metzger, "Jesus' parables were governed by a single purpose—to show, directly or indirectly, what God is and what man may become, and to show these things in such a way that they will reach men's hearts if it is possible to reach them at all."[6] This very basic message is at the heart of the parables of Jesus—"The Rule of God" for a person's life.

3. The parables of Jesus can be grouped along certain themes. In his fine book, *Rediscovering The Parables*, Joachim Jeremias demonstrates that the parables "fall naturally into groups"; and he suggests ten groups from his own study.[7] My work differs from the work of Jeremias in that it suggests a different set of groups into which the parables may fall. It is not my purpose to treat the parables in the order of their presentation in the gospels. Instead, I want to examine certain key ideas—perspectives on the rule of God—that continually recur in the teachings of Jesus. Each chapter in this book represents a particular group

6   Bruce M. Metzger, *The New Testament: Its Background, Growth and Content* (Nashville: Abingdon Press, 1965), 144.

7   Joachim Jerimias, *Rediscovering the Parables* (New York: Charles Schribner's Sons, 1966), 54-70.

of parables which focus on a common key idea.

4. The parables of Jesus tell us what we would have never known or figured out. In the story of the Good Samaritan, we learn that sacrificial love is more crucial than being on time to church or attending church at all. In the story of the friend at midnight, we learn that we should never quit asking God, even when we bother him. The story of the two men praying at the temple reveals that rightness with God depends on humility, not doctrinal position. In the story of the mustard seed, we learn to value small beginnings. These stories, unlike fables, are about forgiveness, relationship, hope, meaning and the purpose of your life.

5. The parables of Jesus have surprise endings. A father whose reputation has been dashed, whose fortune was wasted, and whose name has been tarnished forgives the son who did it. When the vineyard workers are paid at the end of the workday, the last ones hired are paid equally to the ones who worked all day. When the widow is overbearing and persistent, nagging gets results. When hidden treasure is found, finders are keepers. When the tax collector prays beside the Pharisee, good guys do win. The mystery of God accounts for much of the surprise—or shock—that we find in the endings of the parables. It's common for a sheep to wander from the flock, but it is unusual for a shepherd to leave the whole flock to search for one sheep. It is no surprise for a person to incur a large debt—but it is surprising to find a banker who forgives such a sum.

6. The parables of Jesus are brief. They seize our attention and hold it. Jesus makes his point quickly, before we can turn him off. He is in and out in a moment. Some of his parables are but a few sentences in length and he tells them quickly. They are vivid, concrete, and even ironic. They are little seed-thoughts ready to germinate. "All experience shows that parables do attract; and when once understood, are sure to be remembered."[8]

7. The parables of Jesus change us. They are repeatable, enduring. "There is a quality in the parables which time and distance cannot dilute or destroy... Many other teachers have told stories that were lively, but he created life."[9] They endure because they deal with truth, not with probabilities or moral contingencies. When we interpret the parables of Jesus, it is crucial to understand the moment or setting in which the parable was first spoken. Jesus tells them to people living in a particular moment in history. What is the chief point that Jesus intends to make? What is the truth that Jesus brings to us? The parables of Jesus reveal the mysteries of God.

---

8   John M'Clintock and James Strong, *Cyclopaedia of Biblical, Theological and Ecclesiastical Literature*, Vol. 7 (New York: Harper and Brothers, 1891), 646.

9   Russell Bowie, "The Parables," *The Interpreters Bible*, Vol. 7, George A. Buttrick, ed., (New York: Abingdon Press, 1951), 167.

When the disciples come to Jesus and ask, "Why do you speak to the people in parables?" he replies:

> The knowledge of the secrets of the kingdom of heaven has been given to you, but not to them. Whoever has will be given more, and he will have an abundance. Whoever does not have, even what he has will be taken from him. This is why I speak to them in parables: Though seeing, they do not see; though hearing, they do not hear or understand (Matthew 13:10-13).

When Jesus speaks of "the mysteries of God", he refers to them as things that were hidden, known only to God, and revealed by God only at his good pleasure. Jesus copies a spiritual truth or mystery in the reality of the natural world. So the parables have become God's special instruments of change. They are different from literary productions, speeches, and figures of speech—all of which call attention chiefly to the ingenuity of man. They call for change.

For nearly two thousand years, men and women have been listening to the parables of Jesus, seeking their meanings, and drawing near to their truths. Garrison Keillor, America's foremost storyteller, writes, "I think people do want to hear the Gospel in the form of a story.

There's a story at the heart of every sermon."[10] Joyce Huggett writes, "The reason we need to delve into the story and contemplate the picture is that a parable has one single purpose: not to inform the mind but to elicit a response of the heart."[11] Let's take our journey through the parables. One thing is for sure—they will astonish us!

Questions for Discussion

■ START TALKING

☐ What is your favorite movie, TV sitcom, soap opera or (if you'll admit to being old enough to remember) classic radio drama? Even in comic strips, a story line is often featured. Why?

☐ Who is your favorite storyteller? What makes a storyteller effective?

☐ Share with your group one of your favorite parables of Jesus and explain why you especially like it.

■ ENCOUNTERING THE PARABLES

☐ This chapter contains several definitions for a parable:
- an earthly story with a heavenly meaning
- how daily life intersects eternal truth

---

10 Garrison Keillor, "Caught Reading," *Christian Century*, April 10, 1996, 389.

11 Joyce Huggett, *Praying the Parables* (Downer's Grove, Illinois: InterVarsity Press, 1996), 23.

How would you define, in your own words, the parables of Jesus?

☐ React to this statement from Fred Craddock: [A parable] "... draws the listener into personal involvement, and leaves the final resolution of the issue to the hearer's own judgment." What do you think Craddock means? Think of a favorite parable and how it helped you resolve a life issue.

■ BRINGING IT HOME

☐ Recall that the parables of Jesus were transmitted orally for many years before they were written down. Furthermore, many of the parables of Jesus have surprise endings. Do any of Jesus' parables astonish you? Share an illustration of one that does and explain why.

☐ The parables change us. Has anyone in your group experienced growth or spiritual maturity because of a parable from Jesus? Allow at least one group member to share the connection between his/her spiritual transformation and a particular parable.

2

When Heaven Laughs

Bill Peach was born in 1936 in rural Boston, Tennessee. As an 8-year-old boy, he writes about life in middle Tennessee as he remembers it in his book *The South Side of Boston.* Delightfully irreverent in his memories, Peach captures the humor in his early religious experiences.

Mister McLemore Hardison said he had read his Bible, cover to cover, Genesis to Revelation, twenty-one times. People laughed about Mister Hardison because he cussed all the time, and said things that were not nice to women, and was always in a fight with one of his neighbors, and made his wife work in the fields till she got old and sick. Cousin Herbert said Mister Hardison should have read his Bible a little slower, and not so many times, and might have learned to do better. (p.49)

"God has made laughter for me; everyone who hears will laugh over me," said Sarah. But the beginning of Isaac is not the beginning of humor. Even at creation, God gives laughter. Think outside the box. Imagine the first encounter of Adam and Eve. They laugh at their amazement, their joy, their celebration, their discovery, or their mystery. It's perfect joy, ultimate celebration— Eden.

Did you know that heaven laughs? The comic, humorous themes of the Bible tell how the self-righteous religious folks are turned aside at the door. And guess who is admitted? Sinners! If you missed the punch line of that joke, you missed the point as well.

In his excellent book on God and humor, Conrad Hyers observes, "Who wants to make sense or money all the time? ... Laughter is fundamentally an act of celebrating existence. Laughter is an expression both of enjoyment and of thanksgiving. Thus laughter, humor, and comedy are commonly associated with feasting, parties, reunions, weddings, birthdays, spring rites— wherever people get together and say yes to life, in spite of its difficulties and it darker side" (*And God Created Laughter*, 14-15).

Did you know that heaven laughs? The comic, humorous themes of the Bible tell how the self-righteous religious folks are turned aside at the door. And guess who is admitted? Sinners! If you missed the punch line of that joke, you missed the point as well.

Some imagine God as totally humorless:

dour, grave, somber, even vindictive. Yet, this view of God serves better as a definition of sanctimoniousness and a cause for religious hypocrisy. It comes out of ignorance rather than superstition. For instance, not only does the nation of Israel begin in humor—old Abraham and Sarah are going to have a baby and his name will be Isaac (Laughter)—but heaven laughs, also.

The One enthroned in heaven laughs
(Psalm. 2:4)

God laughs at fear, afraid of nothing
(Job 39:22)

But the Lord laughs at the wicked
(Psalm. 37:13)

Nowhere is Scripture clearer about the laughter of heaven than in three stories of Jesus. In narratives marked by the stress of pairing the holy with the unholy, Jesus three times emphasizes how a man from God belongs with rogues, rascals, and racketeers (Lk. 15:1-2). The point: What is it that really matters to God?

One place to start is with three different sets of images: sheep and shepherds, coins and lamps, and fathers and sons. We are about to be treated to the humor of God—heaven laughing over finding a lost sheep, a lost coin, or a lost boy.

Sheep and Shepherds *(Luke 15:1-7)*

The shepherd in the Palestinian hills and plains grazes his sheep very early in the morning—4:00 A.M. would not be unusual. As the sun rises, the shepherd leads his flock to the desert to find green plants. At midday, he waters his sheep, and by evening, he guides them to a safe place of rest. Psalm 23 portrays the shepherd's care, concern, and duty.

Sheep are timid, docile animals that are responsive to affection. Because sheep are not good swimmers, they are afraid of rushing waters. They see only a few feet ahead and have no vision of distant objects. Sheep are utterly defenseless. Who has ever been attacked by a sheep? For sheep to stray is quite common, for they have no sense of direction. Unlike a horse or a dog, which will find its way home when lost, a sheep only seems to wander further away from the flock.

When lost, sheep do not run wildly across creek beds and wilderness plains. They seem to have a lack of initiative, for they lie down and put their legs underneath their bodies. When defenseless and lost, sheep crouch close to the ground.[1]

A shepherd follows an occupation as old as

---

1 For background information on sheep, see J.D. Douglas, ed., *The New Bible Dictionary* (Grand Rapids: Eerdmans Publishing Co., 1975), 1174; Merrill C. Tenney, ed., *The Zondervan Pictorial Bible Dictionary* (Grand Rapids: Zondervan Publishing House, 1963), 44.

Abel (Gen. 4:2). He is responsible for the welfare of his flock. He must find for them grass and water, protect them against attack, and seek any stray sheep (Ps. 23; Amos 3:12; Ezek. 34:8). It is a common practice for shepherds to give names to their sheep and to call to them at regular intervals, reassuring them of their shepherd's presence. Sheep know their shepherd's voice but may run in the other direction at a stranger's call.

A typical Palestinian shepherd counts his sheep several times during the day and night to be sure that none is lost. Under some circumstances, he must make restitution for sheep he cannot find (Gen. 31:39). Thus, the nature of sheep and the duty of a shepherd make retrieval of the lost a continued necessity.

Leaving his flock with other shepherds, a shepherd will begin a search that may take him through thick brush, into caves, and through streams. When he finds the lost sheep, the shepherd calls to him, runs his hands and arms under the belly of the sheep, and then places him gently on his shoulders. With a sense of satisfaction, he returns the lost one to the flock.[2]

Lost Sheep (Luke 25:1-7)

Tax collectors, sinners, and other undesirable people of the land gathered around Jesus. To closely associate with the people of

---

2   For additional reading on shepherds, note Joachim Jeremias, *Rediscovering the Parables* (New York: Charles Scribner's Sons, 1966), 105-106.

Galilee, Jesus might break kosher and become unclean. Unholy crowds in on holy: sin in the presence of God. Thus, the religious leaders charged, "You welcome sinners, and you eat with them." In answer, Jesus tells a story. Here, in essence, he says:

A shepherd had a moderate-sized flock of a hundred sheep. Now, you shepherds know how a flock must be counted at regular intervals. Well, this shepherd found that one of the sheep, one of the unthinking, dependent sheep, had strayed away from the flock. And do you know what he did? He left the flock of ninety-nine and began to search for the one lost sheep. He looked behind bushes and in caves, calling the name of the sheep. He searched and searched. Then, he saw the sheep—frightened, crouched close to the ground, alone, and defenseless. The shepherd picked him up just as some of you shepherds pick up your lost sheep. He ran his hands and arms under the belly of the sheep, put him over his neck, and carried him on his back. After he had returned to his flock, the shepherd called his friends and neighbors together and said, "I want you to share my good news with me. I lost one of my sheep. I searched, looked, and called. I found him. He was lost, and I found him."

After telling the story, Jesus tuned to his accusers. In effect, he told them, "That's what

God is like." As sheep, by nature, have trouble comprehending the shepherd, so we have difficulty understanding God and his ways. God searches for straying, unthinking, misguided, and aimless people. His concern leads to an endless search. He is, as described by 19th-century poet Francis Thompson, "The Hound of Heaven." He finds them and brings them home. Jubilation reigns in his heart when he recovers his lost possession. Heaven laughs because hell weeps. Heaven laughs because salvation works and the Enemy is defeated. Yes, that is what God is like— God laughs when he sees unthinking, dependent, defenseless people come to him.

Coins And Lamps *(Luke 15:8-10)*

Parables are like mirrors in which we can see ourselves.[3] This next story centers on a coin, the *drachma*, which appears only in Luke 15:8 in the New Testament. In American currency, it is equivalent to sixteen cents. One hundred *drachmas* equal a *mina*, and six thousand *drachmas* make up one *talent*. A *drachma* equals a day's wage and is the Greek counterpart to a Roman *denarius*.[4] Among the Jews, a woman covered her head with a *kaffiyeh* or head cloth made of substantial material and set with ornaments or jewelry. If she married, coins that made up her dowry covered the entire front of

---

3   Archibald M. Hunter, *Interpreting the Parables* (Philadelphia: The Westminster Press, 1960), 10.

4   Douglas, op. cit., 840.

her head covering.[5] Even today, women of the Middle East may be seen wearing a string of coins as a part of their headdress.

Even though a bride may receive many gifts, none of her gifts have the symbolic significance of her headdress of coins.

> She will wear them hooked with little hooks into her hair at the wedding ceremony, and she must guard them with her life thereafter ... According to Eastern thinking, if a woman loses one of her ten pieces of silver, God has withdrawn favor from the household, and the blessings which they formerly had have been lost. If she cannot find the coin, she will have to be put out in the street, an outcast; put to die![6]

Her precious coin must be found! So she lights a lamp, and the search begins.

While lamps are frequently mentioned in the Bible, no description of them appears in Scripture. A great variety of lamps for domestic use have been found in Palestine. They are usually made of terra-cotta and bronze. Typically, a household lamp of the Hellenistic period (first century B.C.-A.D.) is like a shallow saucer that

5   Tenney, op. cit., 227.

6   K.C. Pillal, *Light Through An Eastern Window* (New York: Robert Speller and Sons, 1963), 6-7.

holds oil.[7] Jews apparently burned lamps during daylight hours because of the small amount of light entering the door. At night, they burned lamps both to keep away intruders and because of their fear of darkness.

Her coin may have fallen into a hole in the floor, into a corner, or even beneath dust. Floors in the homes of the rich were typically stone slab, while the poor lived upon floors of beaten clay. Hopefully, her broom would hit the coin and bring it to view. Her search could become a long process because, though Palestinian houses were usually small, they were also crowded with furniture, cooking utensils, and clothing.

The Lost Coin (Luke 15:8-10)

Jesus again addressed his critics and said, "Let me tell you a story."

A woman had ten silver coins. While in her house one day, she realized that she had lost one of her coins. This neglected coin became the object of her search. She lit a lamp and began to sweep. She swept in the dark corners, in the crevices of the floor, and around the furniture. She swept, hoping that if she hit the coin it would turn up on the floor. But she didn't find it, so she kept searching and sweeping. And, then, she hit it with her broom. She found her coin! And do

---

7   Tenney, op. cit., 475.

you know what she did next? She called her
friends and neighbors together and said, "You
know my dowry and how important it is to
me. I lost one of my coins, but I lit a lamp,
searched for it, and I found it. That's why I
had to share the good news with you."

Jesus then turned to his accusers and in
essence said, "That's what God is like." He
searches for people who are lonely and lost, for
people looking for their identity, and for people
out of relationship. God never gives up; and
every time he finds one who is lost, heaven
laughs.

Fathers And Sons (Luke 15:11-32)

When God first gave Israel their land, they
believed that it should remain in the family.
Consequently, a basic law of inheritance
developed: the family possesses the land, rather
than a private individual. Since wills were not
known in Judaism before the time of Herod, an
inheritance could be received either upon the
death of one's father or else by a gift.[8] The law of
Moses dictated that the right of inheritance
belonged only to the sons of a legal wife (Deut.
21:15-17; Num. 27:8-11). The eldest son would
receive a double portion, and the others received
equal shares of the estate. Prior to the law of
Moses, however, patriarchs would often favor a

---

8   Douglas, op. cit., 562; Jeremias; op. cit., 101-102

younger son over the firstborn. Examples include Abraham, Isaac, Jacob, and Joseph. The younger son could request possession of his share of the estate and turn it into cash.

While living in a foreign culture, the younger son degraded his inheritance, his values, and his religion by working with unclean animals. Leviticus outlined numerous ceremonial defilements that would make purification necessary. Only the ceremonially clean person might approach God in worship (Exod. 19:10; 30:18-21). Having cut himself off from God in worship, the young boy stood in deep need of cleansing. It was common for a person who saw his or her need of cleansing to pray in the manner of David:

> Cleanse me with hyssop, and I will be clean; wash me, and I will be whiter than snow... Create in me a pure heart, O God, and renew a steadfast spirit within me... A broken and contrite heart, O God, you will not despise (Psalm 51:7, 10, 17).

As a sign of reconciliation, a Jewish father might kiss his son to restore their relationship (2 Sam. 14:33). "The best robe" would signify an occasion of festivity. More costly than the daily, ordinary robe and usually white in color, this robe might be decorated with jewels or bright scarlet and purple sashes. For the father to present a signet ring would represent a restoration of power and position to his son. If the young boy bared his feet, it would signal his destitution and degradation because sandals were considered the lowliest articles of clothing among the people of Palestine (Mark 1:7). Sandals for his bare feet, together with a robe and ring, would definitely demonstrate that the father has restored his son to "sonship."

The Lost Boy (Luke15:11-32)

So again Jesus in essence said, "Let me tell you a story."

The younger boy came to his father and said, "Father, I want you to give me my inheritance of your estate today. I don't want to wait any longer. I have big plans, Father. I have places to go and things to do. And I want my share of your property today."

So the father gave the younger son his part of the inheritance. The young man sold it for cash, took his money, and went on a long trip. He began to drink heavily and found some women who thought he was great as long as he could pay for everything.

Inevitably, one day he reached down in his robe and found no more coins! Dead broke, he turned to begging, but since no one would give him anything to eat, the young boy had to begin to feed hogs—a job considered the lowest of the low and a violation of the Sabbath and the law. Now at the point where eating with pigs looked pretty good, he remembered what it was like back home—the joy, the peace, the sense of belonging, the relationship. "I still have a father," he said, "I'll go back home!"

So he started the long journey back, which took many days. In walking, he became dirtier and dirtier and began to realize that he simply had no case to present to his father The young man had already received everything that belonged to him; his father owed him absolutely nothing. Finally, he neared the house where he had been born and raised. He looked up and saw his father running to meet him! When they got home, his father put a robe on his back, a ring on his finger, and sandals on his feet. His father told everyone, "This is my son who has been lost, and today he has come home to me!"

But that's not the end of the story. The older son heard the merriment. He looked in and saw that his rebellious brother had now returned—his brother who had no right to anything, who had taken their father's money and spent it, and who now wore the honorary robe, ring, and sandals. The elder brother stormed up to his father and complained, "I have been with you all this time working and never disobeying an order. I've done everything you asked me to do, and you have never once given me a party. And now this son of yours comes home, and you prepare a calf for him."

One can imagine Jesus, as he came to this part of the story, leaning forward, cupping his hand with his chin in it, and looking directly at his accusers saying, "My son, you are always with me. Everything that belongs to me belongs to you. But we had to celebrate because your brother and my son has come home."

Whatever a person thinks about God largely determines that person's ministry and mission.

And then Jesus might have told his accusers, "That's what God is like. He is concerned and cares for the rebellious, the selfish, and the totally lost person. And when that person responds to God, he will always celebrate! Heaven laughs again!"

The Heart of God

The earthly ministry of Jesus Christ grounded itself in the nature of God. The Jewish religious leaders thought they had a *prima facie* case that Jesus was not who he claimed to be. If he were the Son of God, he would not associate with the unseemly and the rabble of the land. A holy God would associate only with holy people. He would be found at the holy sacrifices in sacred buildings on special days, but never with unclean, secular, and needy people.

Jesus didn't direct these parables so much to people who knew they were sinners as to the self-righteous and pious. They were the ones who had misunderstood the heart of God. They didn't believe that heaven laughs. Through the parables of The Lost Sheep, The Lost Coin, and The Lost Boy, Jesus showed the heart of God is a heart of generosity, love, and compassion. That's the way God is. When Christ rescues and restores, heaven laughs.

Whatever you think about God largely determines your priorities, your commitments, and your lifestyle. If you show a strong concern for lost people—lonely people, hurting people, and guilty people—that begins with an understanding of a God who is concerned about the real needs of people.

Centuries before Christ, David described God and what he is like: "like a father" (Ps. 103:1-13). For David, any other conception of God missed the point. God is our father! Even when we hurt him, he still loves us. When we reflect badly on his name, he still loves us. When we stray or rebel, he still loves us. He searches, sweeps, and runs to meet us because he is filled with compassion!

A No-Nonsense God

The way God acts often doesn't make much sense to us. At first, it doesn't fit our logic, our common sense, or our sense of fairness. Rationally, it would follow that a shepherd should stay with the ninety-nine sheep. A woman would take care of the nine coins she has. A father would not be able to accept a boy who rebels against him. And why laugh? That's why "the message of the cross is foolishness to those who are perishing, but to us who are being saved it is the power of God" (1 Cor. 1:18). It didn't make much sense to people in the time of Jesus, so they tried to get themselves off the hook with hairsplitting questions. And finally, they crucified him. Self-satisfaction makes us look like the Pharisees. We've grown comfortable with the way things are. So these parables may not make any more sense to us today than it did to them. But that's the way God is! Heaven laughs!

It seems too good to be true! We've just never known anyone on earth that has loved us this much or treated us this way. So many have decided that it really is too good to be true, so it can't be true! Religion then becomes, for thousands and thousands of people, not an experience *with* God, who comes to rule in one's life, but a series of discussions *about* God. So many sincere people—lonely and joyless—have never allowed the kingdom to rule in their lives, never allowed a loving God to take away their guilt, doubt, and fear. Yet, Jesus still says to us, "That's the way God is!"

Religion becomes not an experience with God ... but a series of discussions about God

What God Can Do

Human greatness is exclusive, but divine greatness is inclusive. The first step in the story of salvation is God's step. He reaches out to us. In our response, we bring to God a humble and contrite heart (Ps. 51). God wants to release us from the memory, the guilt, and the regret of past sins. God wants us to experience freedom and release from a life of misdirection, worry, neglect, and rebellion.

The thread that runs throughout Scripture is that we are to bring to God a willing and humble heart. No more evasion, no more blaming of circumstances, no more claim of ignorance, and no self-righteousness. We bring only a sense of personal accountability and a willingness to receive God's total forgiveness. Only then can we feel a renovated spirit, a clean heart, and feeling of forgiveness.

The experience of forgiveness allows us to affirm our salvation in Jesus, to forgive other people, and to discover our own gifts or talents that can become our ministries. A life of celebration and worship, service to others, and deep, personal peace will characterize the life of the forgiven. We would then know how it feels to be a sheep who has been brought back to the flock, a coin that has been found, and a boy who has returned to his father. We would know how it feels to be made whole after living broken lives. We would know how it feels to replace merely outward holiness with intimate friendship with God.

We would know how it feels to be made whole after living broken lives. We would know how it feels to replace merely outward holiness with intimate friendship with God.

What is your conception of God? Do you think he is enjoying your misery? Apathetic at your rebellion? Punishing you through your pain? Do you think he satisfies his needs at your expense?

Or, do you see that he satisfies *your* needs at *his* expense (John 3:16)? Do you see God as flowing with forgiving compassion? Do you see that he is the only hope of the hopeless, the despairing, and the totally lost?

"This man welcomes sinners and eats with them," was the accusation of the Pharisees and teachers of the law (Luke 15:2). But Jesus responded that there was a reason why he gathered sinners into his community. There was a reason why caring and sharing would be the main function of his church. There was a reason why man's deepest needs would be fulfilled in Christ.

It's because that's the way God is. He loves to laugh!

Questions for Discussion

█ START TALKING

Find a partner and discuss the following questions:

☐ Does it a surprise you to imagine a God who laughs? Explain your answer. Why do some find God humorless?

☐ In your opinion, who was the most astonished when Jesus first told the stories of the lost sheep, the lost coin, and the lost son? Was it the publicans and sinners (Luke 15:1,2) or their accusers, the Pharisees?

☐ Share and discuss your answers with the rest of the class.

■ ENCOUNTERING THE PARABLES

☐ All three stories—the lost sheep, the lost coin, the lost son—celebrate the recovery of the lost. They reveal the heart of God, the compassionate father. In these parables, what is most difficult for us to imagine or believe? What is the alternative to believing it?

☐ Jesus began his reply to the religious leaders with the story of a sheep and the story of a coin, not the story of two sons. Why do you think he told the stories in this particular order? Whom does the elder brother in the third story represent? Does God want the religious leaders to be a part of his family? Explain your answer.

■ BRINGING IT HOME

☐ React to this statement: "Whatever a person thinks about God largely determines that person's ministry and mission." If that's true, what are the implications for your ministry and mission? Share a bit of your story with the group, allowing opportunities for others to do the same.

☐ This chapter describes some hearers of these parables as persons whose religion "becomes, not an experience with God,

... but a series of discussions about God." Allow your group to place themselves on the continuum between experiencing God or just discussing him.

3

WHAT IF
NO ONE CAME?

Philadelphia. It was a morning like every other morning. The streets looked the same as busy people passed by the shopping bag ladies who were collecting junk. No one paid any attention. The shopping bag ladies were just a usual part of the Philadelphia downtown landscape. In many ways, the morning looked like any other morning.

Then the most unbelievable thing happened! Each of the nine shopping bag ladies received a special invitation from Wannamaker's Department Store to attend a special luncheon on the top floor. One moment, they were social castoffs walking Philadelphia's streets. In the next moment, they were honored guests in a world of silver, crystal, and china. It was a heart-warming scene—a long banquet table filled with delicious vegetables, meats, fresh fruits, cloth napkins, and magnificent candelabras. Laughter filled the room. Joy was the dominant note of the morning. It was unforgettable!

One lady said, "This is the loveliest thing that's happened to me in my life."

Jesus would have understood exactly what this lady means. In fact, he uses a similar occasion to teach one of his most inspirational lessons on "the rule of God."

Ancient banquets

In ancient times, weddings and funerals both featured banquets. Archaeologists have found a tomb in Turkey that gives us a clue to ancient feasts. The occasion was a royal funeral 2700 years ago, when King Midas ruled. Around 700 BC, everyone enjoyed a dinner of barbecued lamb or goat in a spicy stew. They washed down their grief with quite a beverage—a powerful mixed drink of wine, barley beer, and herbs. We now know their menu. You see, they drank so much, they left behind their dishes and drinking cups, which they didn't bother to wash. Scholars at the University of Pennsylvania call these new findings "dramatic, direct evidence of ancient Mediterranean cuisine and culture." ("King Midas's Funeral: Happy Hour at a Tomb," *New York Times*, December 23, 1999, A18.)

Our best description of a Roman banquet is found in the words of Trimalchio, the chief character in Petronius' *The Satyricon*. The story is set in the first century, exactly at the time of Jesus. Trimalchio is a vain, wealthy, good-natured Roman. Having invited several of his good friends, he prepares a wild display of wealth, both in the showing of his home and in the serving of his banquet. Slaves dressed as hunters carry in roasted wild boar while hounds bark at their heels. Trimalchio brags of one of his cooks, "He will make you a fish out of a sow's belly ... a chicken out of a knuckle of pork." Romans preferred a variety of meats and vegetables from various parts of the empire. Venison, peacock, mullet, sole, flamingo tongue, and salted sea urchins combined with eggs, cheeses, peppers, berries, honey, and oil. Cicero's favorite was brains, liver, eggs, and cheese cooked in salt. Roman menus abounded in vegetables, herbs, and spicy sauces. After hours of eating, Romans would often go to the vomitorium and then return for more. This might go on for days.

Banquets also played an important part in weddings among ancient Jews. A marriage ceremony would usually last ten days, and all the neighbors would be invited to celebrate. If any of them were engaged in fasting and prayer, they would be called upon to suspend such activities for the duration of the marriage feast, for they believed God to be present at the marriage ceremony. Jesus referred to this custom in Matthew 9:15 when he said, "How can the guests of the bridegroom mourn while he is with them? The time will come when the bridegroom will be taken from them; then they will fast." "These guests," writes one scholar, "observed the custom of suspending prayer and fasting during the marriage ceremony; but when this is completed, they may then resume any prayers or fasting they had in progress."[1]

Banquets in biblical times were sumptuous festivals. Amos painted a striking portrait of a typical banquet: guests recline on the beds of ivory; they eat portions of lamb and veal; they drink wine and sing songs; they anoint themselves with oil (Amos 6:4-6). In addition to celebrations of marriage, a banquet occupied center stage in other Jewish celebrations. Feasts were provided for sacrifices (Exodus 34:15; Judges 16:23-25), birthdays (Genesis 40:20; Joel 1:4; Matthew 14:6), funerals (Jeremiah 16:7), the laying of foundations for buildings (Proverbs 9:1-5), sheep shearing (1 Samuel 25:2, 36), and the grape harvest (Judges and 9:27). "A banquet always included wine drinking; it was not simply a feast in our sense."[2] A great feast would last for several days. However, the prophets condemned excessive eating and drinking (Isaiah 5:11ff).

At the time of Jesus Christ, a great banquet would draw attention, ceremony, and celebration. The host of the banquet would invite all of his guests long before the beginning of the banquet. Then, on the day and at the hour of the banquet, he would send one or more of his servants to the expected guests with the announcement that the preparations for the feast were complete and that their presence was expected. The second invitation was delivered

---

1 K. C. Pillai, *Light Through an Eastern Window* (New York: Speller and Sons, 1963), 8-9.

2 Stephen Barabas, "Banquet," *The Zondervan and Pictorial Bible Dictionary*, 95.

verbally by the messenger in the master's name. (It's important to recognize that the master sent his second invitation only to those that had already been invited and declared acceptable.) Any action other than acceptance was considered rejection not only of the feast, but of the host as well: "People are bound by every feeling of honor and propriety to postpone all other engagements to the duty of waiting upon their entertainer."[3] When the host completed his preparations for the great banquet, he would send an invitation as follows: "Everything is ready ... come to the wedding banquet" (Matthew 22:4).

The Great Banquet *(Luke 14:15-24)*

A very prominent Pharisee invited Jesus, along with other guests, to a dinner in his home. By this point in his ministry, Jesus had already confronted several of the prevalent attitudes of Phariseeism. As a result, they "carefully watched him." The Pharisees and experts in the Law of Moses tried to find reasons to disprove the claims of Jesus. They placed him under their orthodox magnifying glass, looking for evidence to confirm that he was not the Son of God. On this particular occasion, their legalistic, judgmental actions turned the dinner into a trial. But this time the issue for debate was not a written

---

3 John M'Clintock and James Strong, "Banquets," *Cyclopaedia of Biblical, Theological, and Ecclesiastical Literature*, Vol. 1 (New York: Harper and Brothers, 1891), 635.

argument, but a human being—"a man suffering from dropsy." Dropsy causes a person to become bloated; the body retains abnormal amounts of fluids, sometimes resulting in the inability to walk, a disagreeable odor, and being abnormally overweight. It would seem highly unlikely that a prominent Pharisee would have invited such an embarrassing person to his feast. But invited or not, the man came and everyone could see him. It was the Sabbath; who would respond to help him? Totally unable to coordinate his body and falling in front of all the prominent, the wealthy, and the religious, the poor man appeared foolish!

While the hearts of the legalistic, self-righteous elite weren't moved, the compassionate heart of God was. Jesus reached out, healed the man, and sent him out of the room. The moment was electric: "Suppose your oxen fell in a well on the wrong day—on the Sabbath day. Will you not pull him out?" Silence blanketed the feast, a cold, quiet response to Jesus' question. Jesus looked at the arrangement of the prominent, upstanding, and sophisticated guests seated around the feast table. The wealthy with their robes, jewelry, and turbans sat next to the prominent, who had their credentials of self-importance. Such people shun someone who appears foolish. Jesus listened as they talked about whom they knew, how much they owned, with whom they networked, and about how wise they had become. All around their table, the self-righteous mingled with the pious; the sophisticated mixed with the proud. Suddenly, out of step with the table talk, Jesus addressed the self-deceived: "When you are invited to a wedding feast, do not sit in the place of honor. Take the low seat. For every one who exalts himself will be humbled, and he who humbles himself will be exalted."

Now to his uncomfortable, prominent guests, Jesus gives the mark of true spirituality: "When you give a feast, invite the poor, the crippled, the lame, and the blind; and you will be blessed. Invite those who cannot repay you, and you will be repaid at the resurrection of the righteous."

One self-righteous guest heard Jesus and then piously claimed to be on God's side: "What a great blessing it will be to enter into God's messianic Kingdom and to accept it." Jesus, knowing that none of those around the table grasped the nature of the rule of God in a person's life, replied, in essence, "Let me tell you story."

A man announced a great banquet and invited many of his close, personal friends, including the prominent, the landowners, the wealthy, and the well-connected. Then, he began extensive preparations for his feast according to the proper customs:

• he prepared the meal and selected the choice wines

• he secured new and costly robes for his guests as a token of his personal esteem and appreciation

- he arranged for the seating of his honored guests around his table
- he secured the finest oil for anointing the guests, their robes, and their beards
- he gathered the most beautiful garlands of flowers for decoration
- he prepared the music, selected the singing, and prepared the dancing

His preparations were the finest. The feast was ready for celebration.

As is the well-known custom, the host sent his servant to announce, "Come, everything is now ready for the great feast." As the master's servant gave this second invitation to a guest, he listened to the response and couldn't believe it: "I can't come. I'm just too busy in my new business to come to the feast. I just bought a new field to go with all my other holdings. And I really need to spend some time looking at my new purchase. Please ask your master to excuse me."

So the master's servant went to another already invited guest and invited him again. But the guest said, "I can't come. I'm too overwhelmed with my work. I just bought oxen to go with my other flocks and herds. I need to find out how strong and how hard working they are. Tell your master I would really like to come. But I can't today."

So the servant continued to go from guest to guest inviting, for the second time, his master's friends to the great banquet. Still another guest told him, "I just can't come. You see my wife and I just married and we're in love. We just can't break away from each other. There's no way I can come to your master's feast and take time to be at the banquet. Please excuse me."

So the servant went back to his master with his head down and reported, "You're not going to believe this! Not a guest is coming! Not one of the people you invited will be here. When you serve dinner, there will not be anyone at the table." The owner of the house then became angry and instead of inviting the powerful, rich, and influential, he ordered his servant to invite people like the man with the dropsy. "Go out quickly into the streets and alleys of the town and bring in the hurting, the lame, the lonely, the guilty, the blind, the street people, the prostitutes, and the not-so-good people of the land. Go out to the countryside and persuade them to come in so my house will be full. Not one of those men who were invited will get a taste of my banquet."

A Royal Wedding Banquet
(Matthew 22:1-14)

In the ancient world, banquets took days to prepare but royal weddings took months. The king would use large numbers of people and their skills and talents to prepare for the wedding.

Prior to the wedding, he would host a special wedding banquet, which drew a large guest list. The king usually invited representatives from other nations as well as the rich and powerful from his own nation. It was a choice invitation.

At the heart of the invitation was a special wedding robe, designed for a royal occasion; it was a special, much-desired gift from the king. During the Roman period, garments such as robes were symbols of rank and station and were usually marked by distinctive insignia. A robe with the royal seal would be sent to the home of a guest a day or two in advance of the wedding. Each guest, then, would be assured of being properly attired for the occasion.[4] Attending a royal wedding without wearing a wedding robe would be a serious breach of custom. In fact, it would be totally insensitive and unimaginable for guest to wear his own clothes in the place of a royal wedding robe.

How could a guest enter such a splendid occasion without wearing any kind of wedding robe? Well here's one explanation that helps us to understand the process of entrance into a royal wedding banquet:

When guests arrive for the wedding, they come first to a sort of porch. A tub of water and a servant are provided so that the guests may wash their feet after having walked in the dusty pathways. The servant holds a very humble and lowly position in the household and would have no authority to challenge a guest who might

---

4 K.C. Pillai, op. cit., 14.

come without a robe. After washing their feet, the guests pass into a room where another servant awaits. The task of this servant is to sprinkle rose water on the head and body of the guest. He, like first servant, has no authority to challenge a guest who might not properly be attired.[5]

If, for any reason, a guest willfully refused to wear the royal robe, he might properly be dismissed from the banquet. Knowing that his audience understood this custom, Jesus seems to say again, "Let me tell you a story."

Once there was a king who prepared a formal wedding banquet for his son. He sent out all the invitations, prepared the menu, selected the wines, and looked forward with great anticipation to the marriage feast. At just the right moment, the king sent out his servants with the message, "We're going to have a great banquet. My son is getting married. Everything is ready, so come to the wedding feast."

But they paid no attention to his invitation. Some even abused and murdered the king's servants. The king was so shocked and enraged that he sent out his army, destroyed the murderers, and burned their city. "The banquet is ready. You're to go out and urgently appeal to people to come to my son's wedding feast. Go the street corners and wherever you find people, invite them to our

5 Ibid, 14-15.

royal wedding feast."

The banquet hall was filled with all kinds of people: both men and women, young and old, rich and poor, and various ethnic groups. When the King entered, he looked around the see who had accepted his invitation. Suddenly he stared in shock at a man seated at the end of one of the tables. The man was without a royal wedding robe. The king ordered him thrown out of the banquet hall.

A God Who Doesn't Need Our Help!

Jesus wants us to let God be God! Sometimes religious people want to decide who is at the table and who is not. Too bad! God doesn't require help. It is God who invites, not we. Salvation begins with God, not us! God is the subject of salvation in the Bible and we are the objects. Self-righteousness has a hard time with God's sovereignty.

So, God is the great host! He is the one who invites, prepares, plans, and saves. Anyone who eats at the Messianic banquet table is not there because of who he is, but because of who God is. You and I are not at the table because of our good works, our piety, our importance, or our right doctrine, but because we accept the invitation of God. "For many are invited, but few are chosen."

What A Robe!

God offers us his royal wedding garment of salvation, forgiveness, and relationship.

Clothing symbolizes God's gift to us—our acceptance in Christ. So one day he invited an African riding in his chariot in the desert to the table and he put on the robe. God offered his invitation to a jailer in the middle of the night and he wore the robe. He invited a successful businesswoman in Philippi and she put on the robe. He even invited Saul, who was on a mission to kill Christians, and he wore the robe. You may not think you're eligible to be at the table, but by wearing Jesus Christ, you are graciously invited to be at the party. In fact, God wants every person to wear Jesus Christ as his wedding robe to the banquet table. "For all of you who were united with Christ in baptism have been clothed with Christ" (Galatians 3:27). In both the Old and New Testaments, a robe symbolizes the redeemed community (Isaiah 61:18; Revelation 3: 4-5, 18). Our own homemade clothes won't admit us. If we try to come into his presence dressed in our own righteousness instead of his free gift of grace, the result is banishment from the table.

Surprise! Surprise!

Look around—you'll be surprised at who will be sitting next to you. You may have your own idea of the seating arrangement, but God is the great host. It may not make sense to you, may surprise you, may perplex you, may even anger you, but God has his own plans for his great celebration party.

As you look around, you may find some astonished faces quite surprised to see you at the table. You may even be surprised to be there too! But God is the great host! As long as you are wearing Jesus Christ, you have an invitation to be at the table. Live in a daily wonder that you're invited. Don't take your invitation for granted nor think that you deserved it. Wear your robe of Jesus proudly as you come into the presence of God. Forgiven people sit at the King's banquet table. No longer gripped by the spiritual paralysis of guilt, we are forgiven and able to celebrate joyously. He's invited you to heaven's party!

What a Party!

Questions for Discussion

■ START TALKING

☐ Find three partners. Find out who has a story of the most unusual or memorable invitation to a party, event, or happening. What made this person's story so amazing? Share the story with the rest of the group.

■ ENCOUNTERING THE PARABLES

☐ Why would an uninvited person want to

attend a banquet? Why would the person risk the social stigma of being an uninvited guest?

☐ Jesus intended these two parables to astonish his listeners. What was the most surprising aspect of the stories, in your opinion? Were the uninvited guests subject to the rule of God? In what sense did God invite them to the banquet? Why might this outcome have been surprising to Jesus' hearers?

☐ Compare the reactions of these hearers: the man with dropsy, the Pharisees, Jesus' enemies, and the early church. Would the earliest Christians have been disturbed by these stories?

■ BRINGING IT HOME

☐ What motivates people to accept God's offer of salvation in Jesus Christ? Why would people today risk coming to God's banquet, even though "uninvited"?

☐ What message of these parables seems astounding to you? Whom do you know that might be astounded by these two parables?

☐ How does God extend his invitation through you and me? Brainstorm ways we might support and encourage one another to allow God to use us for extending his grace and mercy in our marriages, families, neighborhoods, work places, and congregations.

4

TAKES MORE THAN GOOD FENCES TO MAKE GOOD NEIGHBORS

Do you like ice hockey? If so, take your seat in the Reading hockey rink, north of Boston. Thomas Junta, a 42-year-old truck driver, is there too. He's there to watch his 10-year-old son play. The game is rough and it's filled with collisions, known as body checking, that only young bodies can withstand. Perhaps Junta wishes his son could someday play in the National Hockey League. Perhaps he wants to see his son win a college scholarship to play hockey. Whatever the reason, he soon becomes embroiled with 40-year-old Michael Costin, father of a player on the other team. Costin is monitoring play on the ice and Junta starts screaming at him to stop some of the body checking and fighting that involves their 10-year-old sons. As Costin leaves the rink, Junta slams him to the ground by a soda machine. Costin's head hits the concrete floor. Junta pushes his knee into Costin's chest and pummels him in the head. Costin dies. Authorities charge Junta with manslaughter.

What lies behind such violence toward another human being? William Pollack of the

Harvard Medical School suggests that more parents are directing their children to play more aggressively. Bob Still of the National Association of Sports Officials says, "There is definitely a trend." Still tells of a coach, the father of a player, who broke the jaw of a 13-year-old umpire at a Little League game in Davie, Florida. Fred Engh of the National Alliance for Youth Sports says that many parents are saying, "My child is going to get some of that money, the millions of dollars in professional sports or a college scholarship." (*The New York Times*, July 11, 2000, A14)

It's called "road rage." A survey of 10,000 drivers in sixteen European countries shows that British motorists have intense road rage and are the first to demonstrate their anger. The worst are the White Van Men, so named because of their vehicles. They see the road as their own, make up their own traffic rules, curse other drivers, and threaten their lives. They are called "folk devils" according to Peter Marsh, Director of England's Social Issues Center. Fights usually begin at traffic lights. White Van Men view the highway as their own turf, not belonging to others.

We live next door to some good neighbors. When we're away, they pick up the mail and the papers. They're friendly, thoughtful, and caring. We've known them for more than ten years. Recently, we built a new fence, which we share. We split the cost of the fence and we're both pretty proud of that fence. But there's more to being a good neighbor than sharing a fence!

Jesus uses the notion of "neighbor" to tell us how we can be absolutely certain that God rules our life. In two of his stories, he stresses what it means to be a "neighbor." His stories: the Good Samaritan and the rich man and Lazarus.

Priests, Levites, And Samaritans

The seventeen-mile road from Jerusalem to Jericho was known to be dangerous. The lonely, narrow road of Jesus' day twisted through the Judean hills down to Jericho. In ancient days, just as in modern times, robberies frequently took place on the Jericho road. It was in a time where little value was given to human life; it was not unusual for a person to be found on the Jericho road, stripped, beaten, and half-alive.

Priests were the descendants of Aaron and, beginning with the time of David, were organized into twenty-four orders (1 Chron. 24:1-19). Even though priests were assigned to various cities, such as Jericho, each order of the priesthood served in the temple two weeks of each year.

The sons of Levi were consecrated as helpers for the priests. These Levites were divided into three families, each having specific duties. The principal function of the Levites was in the rituals of cleansing and dedication (Num. 8:5ff).[1]

---

1   For additional background reading on priests and Levites, see D.A. Hubbard, "Priests and Levites," *The New Bible Dictionary* (Grand Rapids: William B. Eerdmans Publishing Company, 1975), 1028-1034.

Why, then, would a priest not help a person in need? He may have been unsure whether the victim was dead or alive, and ritual forbade a priest to touch a dead body (Lev. 21:11). Of course, the priest simply might have been in a great hurry—too busy to reach out to human needs! Whatever may have been his reason, the Levite did not reach out to the needs of the man in the ditch. As Lightfoot stresses, "Thus the priest and the Levite by their occupations recognize the claims of God, but in their lives they fail to recognize the claim of humanity."[2]

A history of bitterness and resentment marked the relationship between Jews and Samaritans. In 722 B.C. the Assyrians deported the leading citizens of Israel. Those Jews whom the Assyrians left in the land intermarried with non-Jews. During the period of the rebuilding of the temple, the Samaritans opposed the Jews, perhaps only for political reasons. By the time of Nehemiah, the feelings between the Jews and Samaritans were running strong and deep. By the time of Jesus, feelings were at an all-time low. "Between A.D. 6 and 9," one scholar writes, "Samaritans scattered bones in the Jerusalem temple during a certain Passover."[3] With this desecration, animosity intensified. Jews called Samaritans "dogs" and would cross the Jordan River on foot rather than travel through Samaria. Proud of their racial heritage, Jews looked upon

---

2   Neil R. Lightfoot, *Lessons From The Parables* (Grand Rapids: Baker Book House, 1965), 65.

3   Hubbard, op. cit., 1132.

the Samaritans as traitors and heretics. What a shock to a Jew, then, that Jesus would choose a Samaritan as a person of compassion. How can you be a neighbor to your enemy?

The Good Samaritan (Luke 10:25-37)

A sharp lawyer tested Jesus by engaging him in a philosophical discussion on the bounds and limits of being a neighbor. Wanting to justify himself, the lawyer asked Jesus, "And who is my neighbor?" In reply, Jesus told him a story.

A man traveled the seventeen miles between Jerusalem and Jericho. As he traveled along his way, robbers rushed out from the ditch and behind the rocks. They stole his money and his clothes and beat him up, leaving him almost dead. After a while a priest happened to be going down the same road. He heard moans of pain, anguish, and cries for help. He saw the half-alive man lying in the ditch beside the road. Do you know what the priest did? He kept on walking! After a while a Levite, a helper in the temple, came upon the beaten, half-dead man. He, too, kept on walking. traveling the same seventeen miles, a Samaritan came upon the half-alive Jew. This Samaritan, however; saw the injured man's urgent needs and was moved with compassion. He stopped and got down into the ditch beside the man. He disinfected the wounds and carefully bandaged them. He

then lifted the man upon his donkey and tenderly held him all the way to the Jericho inn. The next day he took out two days' wages and gave them to the innkeeper saying. "Look after him; and when I return, I will reimburse you for any extra expense you may have."

Which of these people was a true neighbor? The expert in the law apparently couldn't bring himself to dirty his lips by saying the word "Samaritan" and so responded, "The one who had mercy on him!" Jesus replied, "You go and do likewise."

Beggars And Rich People

In the Old Testament, relieving the need of a beggar was considered a personal virtue. The New Testament also has a great deal to say about material possessions. Since poor people tend to look beyond themselves for guidance and direction in their lives, they were attracted to Jesus in great numbers (Luke 4:18). Through his message and his life, Jesus stressed the importance of meeting the needs of the poor and those in need.

The contrast between rich and poor was vivid in Jesus' time. The sight of a crippled, diseased, and hungry beggar was tragic but common. Jesus could well have seen street dogs licking the sores of a beggar sitting at the gate of a rich man's mansion. In ancient times, those who ate sumptuously at a rich man's table would dip pieces of bread in their dish, wipe their hands on the bread, and throw it under the table.[4] Beggars often scrambled for these pieces of bread.

The rich lived in sharp contrast to the beggar in the street. Playboy types were known in the time of Christ—those who surrounded themselves with all the luxury of high living. Often wearing Egyptian "royal linen" and purple robes of honor and wealth, a rich man had the finest of everything.[5] With his wealth came all the expressions of fine living, along with the temptation to depend upon himself rather than God. After all, he had contacts; he knew his way around; he could solve his own problems.

The Rich Man And Lazarus *(Luke 16:19-31)*

Jesus told a parable about wealth and dependence upon God.

There was a wealthy man who dressed in the finest clothes, ate from a bountiful table, lived in a very comfortable house with all the luxuries, and spent his time satisfying his own desires. He had a great fortune and used it for himself. But at the doorstep of his mansion laid a beggar named Lazarus. He was

---

4 Joachim Jeremias, *Rediscovering The Parables* (New York: Charles Scribner's Sons, 1966), 146.

5 F.C. Fensham, "Linen," *The New Bible Dictionary*, pp. 740-741; Lightfoot, op. cit., 134.

diseased, crippled, and so hungry that he wished to eat the pieces of bread that the rich man threw under his table. Roaming street dogs came and licked the running sores of Lazarus' body.

But the time came when both of them died. The beggar took his place with the righteous, but the rich man took his place with those separated from God's presence. The rich man begged Abraham, who was beside Lazarus, for compassion and ease. But Abraham replied, "Remember that in your lifetime you had good things, but you lacked kindness and compassion. On earth Lazarus received bad things, but his humility and faithfulness are now rewarded." The rich man, then, pleaded for an opportunity for his five brothers to be warned about eternity. Abraham replied, "They have Moses and the prophets; and if they will not listen to them, they'll not be convinced if someone rises from the dead."

To be surrounded with abundance and luxury and ignore those in need misses the point about life in the kingdom. Lack of compassion, pity, and feeling for those in deep need demonstrates a total absence of the rule of God in one's life. Worship attendance, religious acts, and gifts to charities should not be mistaken for being a neighbor.

Kingdom Ethics

In these two parables Jesus becomes very practical. He starts "meddlin'." Instead of challenging our heads, he engages our lives. That's why these stories make us uncomfortable. As Lightfoot comments,

> It gets down to the bottom of what Christianity really is. There is not room for pious platitudes and hair-splitting definitions, no place for Christianity in the abstract or for a religion to be seen of man. With one scene that flashes upon the screen, Jesus compels us to see that Christianity is a way of living.[6]

The ethic of Jesus must translate into action. "After all," writes D. Martyn Lloyd-Jones, "The Law was not meant to be praised, it was meant to be practiced. Our Lord did not preach the Sermon on the Mount in order that you and I might comment upon it, but in order that we might carry it out."[7]

How do you carry it out? Are not the ethical concerns of those ruled by God the identical concerns of Jesus Christ? But the ethics of Jesus only make sense to those who are in

---

6   Ibid., 65-66.

7   D. Martyn Lloyd-Jones, *Studies in the Sermon on the Mount*, Vol. 2 (Grand Rapids: William B. Eerdmans Publishing Co., 1967), 211.

submission to the lordship of Christ! So, as Jesus fed the hungry, clothed the naked, and ministered to prisoners, he demonstrated the great inward concern of God for the human situation. The Bible does not claim that Jesus came to establish a series of social programs designed to improve or reform society. To reduce the good news of the kingdom of God into a series of social initiatives in the non-Christian world is the same as asking people to accept the ethics of Jesus without accepting his rulership in their lives.

The word of God does not call upon us to make a choice between social concern or personal salvation. It calls for both!

But at precisely this point, some are tempted to walk away from the issue of human concern without feeling a sense of responsibility for the world's needs. Many religious people today still call Jesus "Lord, Lord" (Matt. 7:21-23), lift up his name in respect and worship, yet show no relationship to him by ministering to the needs of others. The word of God does not call upon us to make a choice between social concern or personal salvation. It calls for both! We are truly "Christian" only if our salvation leads us to serve others. It is when we personally respond to the lordship of Christ and allow God to rule our hearts that we then begin to serve the needs of our fellowman. So God says throughout his word that his religion hangs on two commandments: (1) to personally love and serve God, and (2) to love and serve one's fellowman (Deut. 6:4-9).

To love one's neighbor is to serve *anyone* who needs help. So the range of application for the ethic of the kingdom includes everyone. Unconditional love, which is learned from the greatest Lover, will cause us to become servants prepared to be exploited, used, and to show deep feeling for those in need. People still lie beside the road and at our gate. Consider the hungry, the orphans, the disenfranchised, the sick, the jobless, the prisoner, the emotionally ill, the unguided youth, the aged, the unmarried pregnant women, and the dying. Let's not miss the point of our faith: *service to our fellowman comes out of a life ruled by God.* "In everything, do to others what you would have them do to you, for this sums up the Law and the Prophets" (Matt. 7:12). "To obey this commandment a man must become a new man with a new centre to his life ..."[8]

Christianity or Culture

Being a neighbor is being concerned about the real needs of real people! The nature of the Lord's kingdom is not political or social. Jesus says, "My kingdom is not of this world" (John 18:36). Being a neighbor runs counter to the way our world thinks.

Our culture says, "Think of your self first ... Look after number one; if you don't, no one else will ... Protect your rights and privileges ... Just

---

8 William Barclay, *The Gospel of Matthew*, Vol. 1 (Philadelphia: The Westminster Press, 1959), 281.

don't get caught." But the way of Christ shows that an ethic rooted in self is like that of the priest and Levite, who passed by human concern "on the other side of the road" or like that of the rich man, who showed no concern for Lazarus.

In direct contrast to culture, Christ says, "Deny yourself ... Serve others ... Whatever you did for one of the least of these brothers of mine, you did for me." It's another way of saying that Jesus is your neighbor.

Beside The Road

Jesus promises us that when we lay our lives down in service to God and our fellowman, *then* we truly find life.

> I tell you the truth, unless a kernel of wheat falls to the ground and dies, it remains only a single seed. But if it dies, it produces many seeds. The man who loves his life will lose it, while the man who hates his life in this world will keep it for eternal life (John 12:24-25).

Sure, it's hard! It's incredibly hard! No one in Scripture ever said it would be easy. To be a neighbor is to meet people beside the roads of life and out at the gates of life, to be among hurting people who have desperate needs. It's to lay our lives down, wash feet, identify with the pain of people, and find our life.

We always carry around in our body the death of Jesus, so that the life of Jesus may also be revealed in our body. For we who are alive are always being given over to death for Jesus' sake, so that his life may be revealed in our mortal body. So then, death is at work in us, but life is at work in you (2 Corinthians 4:10-12).

A Process And The Product

How are we to be real neighbors? How shall we serve the real needs of real people?

The Bible describes being a neighbor as a process which is shaping us into a final product-the image of Christ. This process is marked by three characteristics:

> *When God comes to rule in the heart of a person, the ethics of Jesus are worked out in his daily life.*

(1) It is an ethic of *specifics*, not generalities.

(2) It is an ethic of *action*, not apathy.

(3) It is an ethic of *compassion*, not self-centeredness.

When God comes to rule in your heart, the ethics of Jesus are worked out in your daily life. It's primarily revealed in the way you treat others not only at home, but at hockey matches and on interstate highways. The process takes time and includes the pain of having to treat others as you would like them to treat you. C.S. Lewis describes the process from Christ's point of view:

> The moment you put yourself in my hands, that is what you are in for. Nothing less, or other, than that. You have free will, and if you choose, you can push Me away. But if you do not push Me away, understand that I am going to see this job through. Whatever suffering it may cost you in your earthly life, whatever incon-ceivable purification it may cost you after death, and whatever it costs Me, I will never rest, nor let you rest, until you are literally perfect—until my Father can say without reservation that He is well pleased with you, as He said He was well pleased with me. This I can do and will do. But I will not do anything less.[9]

Chief Seattle once said, "We didn't create the web. We are but a small part of it."

So, being a neighbor is more than sharing a fence. It includes self-denial, laying down our personal lives in the service of other people, and giving ourselves over to loving God and our

---

9   C. S. Lewis, *Mere Christianity* (New York: Macmillan Co., 1958), 157-158.

fellow man. Sure, it's hard and painful. But we can thank God, the Potter, for shaping us into the very image he has in mind. In the end, we won't even recognize what we look like, for we will look like Christ!

Questions for Discussion

■ START TALKING

☐ Do a quick survey in your small group. Ask for a show of hands: How many believe people today are more neighborly than in the past twenty years?

☐ As those who raised their hands to share the reasons for their belief. Let others who didn't raise their hands explain why they take a differing view.

■ ENCOUNTERING THE PARABLES

☐ The Good Samaritan and the Rich Man and Lazarus are very familiar parables. How has our familiarity with these two stories affected our ability to understand them? Are these parables astonishing, or are they old hat? Explain your answer to the group.

☐ If the victim on the road to Jericho had been killed, what justification might the priest and Levite have had for walking by? Jesus frames this parable with a Samaritan who would have no such restrictions as the priest or the Levite. How is his behavior a model for Christian behavior today?

☐ Do you imagine the lawyer who originally posed the neighbor question anticipated the story Jesus told?

☐ What is so disturbing about the story of the Rich Man and Lazarus? Are concern and compassion electives for Christians? Explain.

■ BRINGING IT HOME

☐ Have we outlawed the Good Samaritan in our litigious society? Should we treat others as he did, even if by doing so we risk litigation?

☐ Can we differentiate our Kingdom ethics from our "natural" compassion and neighborliness? Should we? Do the answers to these questions reveal a need for us to change or do something differently this week?

☐ Close your discussion with a prayer of accountability and confession, as well as requests for God to bless, intercede, and intervene.

5

OKAY!
I'LL ANSWER THE DOOR!

The story goes like this: one night, Jesus tells a man he has work for him to do and shows him a large rock in front of this cabin. The Lord explains that the man is to push against the rock with all his might. So, day after day, the man pushes. After years of pushing against the rock, the man begins to feel that all his work has been in vain. You see, the rock has not moved an inch. Seeing signs of discouragement, Satan tempts the man: "You've been pushing against that rock for a long time and it hasn't budged. Give up. You're never going to move it." So the man begins to get disheartened. He decides to pray. "Lord, I've really worked at this. I've put all my strength into it, but the rock hasn't moved. Why am I failing? What's wrong?"

The Lord responds with love. "My friend, when I asked you to follow me, you accepted. I asked you to push against that rock with all your might and you've done that. Your task was to push. Now you feel like a failure, but look at yourself—strong, lots of muscles, powerful arms and hands. Through adversity, you've become stronger. Yet, you haven't moved the rock. However, your call was to obey me, push against the rock, and trust me. I will now move the rock."

Just P.U.S.H.

• When you don't understand—P.U.S.H.

• When you're discouraged and depressed—P.U.S.H.

• When you're suffering and full of pain—P.U.S.H.

• When you've been rejected, overlooked—P.U.S.H.

By the way—P.U.S.H. stands for Pray Until Something Happens!

Beggars in the Middle East just won't leave you alone. As you walk down a street, step out of a car, begin eating a meal, or enter a hotel, beggars persist in asking you for money.

Jesus applied to his own followers a beggar's wisdom and the man's persistence in pushing the rock. Such persistence impressed Jesus, and he used it to give insight into the grounds on which we might rest our confidence. Of course, it's best understood by listening to his stories.

Judges and Widows

The judges mentioned in the New Testament performed a different function from those mentioned in the Old Testament book of Judges. Israel looked up to her judges as heroes, leaders in battle, and rulers: "... the Lord raised up judges, who saved them out of the hands of these raiders" (Judges 2:16). They acted in place of a king. In New Testament times, however, the Sanhedrin served as the final court of authority for the Jews. Outside of court, an official with authority to pronounce judgment in legal cases served as "judge." Bribing such a judge was common, so the rich and powerful often received no punishment for their wrongdoing. Meanwhile, defenseless widows, orphans, and the handicapped received little or no justice.[1]

The Bible places widows in a special category of concern, compassion, and consideration. The early church was warned to "give proper recognition to those widows who are really in need" (1 Tim. 5:3ff.). A widow was legally defenseless and an object of charity and compassion. The Law and the prophets commanded the people of Israel to give merciful consideration to widows (Deut. 14:29).[2] A

---

1 For additional background reading on the role of a judge, see G.T. Manley, "Judges," *The New Bible Dictionary* (Grand Rapids: William B. Eerdmans Publishing Co., 1975), 676; C.U. Wolf, "Judge," *The Interpreter's Dictionary of the Bible*, Vol. 2 (Nashville: Abingdon Press, 1962), 1012-1013.

2 Barabus, "Widow," *The Zondervan Pictorial Bible Dictionary* (Grand Rapids: Zondervan Publishing House, 1963), 894; O.J. Baab, "Widow," *The Interpreter's Dictionary of the Bible*, Vol. 4, 842.

Jewish widow had no inheritance rights, was exposed to manipulation and harsh treatment, and was not honored for her widowhood.[3] The Old Testament prophets constantly warned Israel against mistreatment of widows and the underprivileged. Numerous biblical warnings would suggest that inferior treatment, injustice, and lack of mercy were usually received by widows. Early Christians did organize a care program for Greek widows (Acts 6:1ff.), for acceptable service to God included serving the needs of widows (James 1:27).

The Persistent Widow (Luke 18:1-8)

Jesus wants his followers to make room for God in their lives. He stresses the many ways God acts in the world, the many ways God can be reached, and the many ways God responds. Jesus emphasizes persistence, so he tells this parable:

A judge who lived in a certain town did not care about people. His verdicts were unjust, and he dispensed justice to those who bribed him. Needless to say, he cared little about God. In that same town, however, there lived a widow who found herself totally defenseless because of her inferior position in the community. She was an object of charity and had absolutely no recourse in a legal settlement, except to throw herself on the

---

3 Loc. cit.

mercy of the judge. One day, this widow was among those who came to the unjust judge for help. She pleaded, "Help me, judge. Please decide in my favor." The judge ignored her pleas, for he didn't care about her or anyone else. But the next time he held court, she came again and pleaded with him, "Please judge, grant me justice against my adversary." Again he ignored her, showing no concern for her problem. The next time his court convened the judge found her before him once again. "Please grant me justice against my opponent," she pleaded. But still he ignored her. Thereafter, each time the judge held court she was there in the room crying and pleading for assistance. Finally, the judge gave up. He reasoned, "The only way to keep this woman from bothering me is to give her what she wants." So he gave her justice.

And then Jesus turns and tells his apostles, "If an inconsiderate, insensitive, and unjust judge can be moved by the persistent pleas of a widow, will not a loving God bring justice to his own people?" Jesus constantly stresses that we serve a King who cares and who can be moved by the pleas of our hearts. God is touched in his very inner being by our guilt, hurts, and lostness. He is not moved by men of standing, but by men of kneeling.

> *He is not moved by men of standing, but by men of kneeling.*

Bread At Midnight

Travel by night is still common in the Middle East due to the intense daytime heat. I have traveled at various times of the day and night in several countries of the Middle East and found that even at night there may be few breezes. So the arrival of a friend at the home of his host in the middle of the night would not be uncommon.

Custom calls for the host to set a full meal before his arriving guests. And the meal might become a community project. Village women cooperate in bread baking, and it is known who has baked most recently. There may be some bread left in the host's house, but he must offer the guest a complete, unbroken loaf. To feed a guest with a partial loaf left from another meal would be an insult.[4] Even today, three full loaves are regarded as necessary for a meal for one person.[5]

The host could be confident that he could borrow from his neighbors to help him feed his guest. This confidence was based upon the fact "that the guest is guest of the *community*, not just of the individual. ... In going to his neighbor, the host is asking the sleeper to fulfill his duty to the guest of the village."[6] Refusal to

---

4 Kenneth F. Bailey, *Poet and Peasant* (Grand Rapids: William B. Eerdmans Publishing Co., 1976), 122.

5 Joachim Jeremias, *Rediscovering the Parables* (New York: Charles Scribner's Sons, 1966), 124.

6 Bailey, op. cit., 122-123.

help in the entertainment of a guest would be unimaginable. Bread at midnight for a guest would be necessary under any circumstances.

The Persistent Host *(Luke 11:5-10)*

After Jesus finished praying one day, his disciples asked him to teach them to pray. Jesus gave them what has come to be called "The Lord's Prayer." Afterwards, he told them a parable that stressed persistence in prayer.

Suppose a man has an unexpected visit in the middle of the night by a friend. Realizing he is the host, suppose the man goes to a neighbor at midnight and breaks the quietness of the night with a loud knock crying, "Friend, lend me some bread to help feed my guest. I don't have enough food to serve him." But suppose the neighbor answers, "Go away, don't bother me. I've already locked the door. Besides, my family is asleep, so I can't get up and give you anything." Now, suppose the host doesn't give up but continues to plead with his neighbor over and over. You know what the neighbor will do, don't you! Because of the man's persistence, the neighbor will get up and give him whatever he needs.

Then Jesus turned to his disciples and explained that they could approach God because he is "our Father." God is not inconvenienced.

So Jesus said:

> Ask and it will be given to you; seek
> and you will find; knock and the door
> will be opened to you. For everyone
> who asks receives; he who seeks finds;
> and to him who knocks, the door will
> be opened (Luke 11:9-10).

Jesus then said it another way. No human
father would trick his own children by giving
them a deadly snake when they asked for bread.
Our perfect father in heaven readily gives the
Holy Spirit to those who ask him (Luke 11:11-
13). Jesus taught that the God to whom we pray
will always be moved by our prayers.

'Okay, I'll answer the door.'

One of the great mysteries of our
relationship to God is how we as finite human
beings can actually affect the infinite God of the
universe. You may think that he is too busy with
big stuff—cosmos, galaxies, earth-shaking events.
Yet, Scripture is alive with examples of the power
of prayer. The stories of intercessory prayer are
the stories of moving God's great heart. Over
and over, God keeps saying, "Okay, I'll answer
the door."

When God decided to destroy the city of
Sodom, Abraham prayed to God for the salvation
of just a few people. His prayer affected God
(Gen. 18:24 ff.) and God answered the door.

When God saw the people of Israel worshiping a golden calf after he had liberated them from Egypt, he decided to destroy them. But Moses prayed to God, and his prayer affected the great heart of God. The people of Israel remained the people of God (Exod. 32:31 ff.). God answered the door.

When Jesus is about to go to the cross, Satan comes to him and makes a devilish request. Jesus reports it as follows: "Simon, Simon, Satan has asked to sift you as wheat. But I have prayed for you, Simon, that your faith may not fail. And when you have turned back, strengthen your brothers" (Luke 22:31-32). God answered the door.

"The prayer of a righteous man is powerful and effective" (James 5:16b).

Why does intercessory prayer affect God? The answer seems to lie in the *nature of God.* If even hardhearted human beings will respond to persistent pleading, begging, and requesting, then God, who cares more than any human being, can be changed by persistent prayer. It is his nature to care, and prayer is fundamentally built upon God's nature. If an insensitive, inconsiderate judge finally gives in to a widow in distress, how much more will God? If a sleepy neighbor, looking out for his own family, heeds a friend's request for bread, how much more will God?

... prayer affects God ... due to the bold confidence of God's deisciples.

Intercessory prayer affects God also because of the *bold confidence of God's disciple.* Jesus stresses in each of these parables the "persistence" of the one pleading. The Greek word for "persistence" is used only this once in the New Testament, and its meaning literally is "lack of shame."[7] We should not think of persistence as nagging or as badgering, which are negative traits. Persistence is constancy and boldness, very positive attributes. "Let us then approach the throne of grace with confidence, so that we may receive mercy and find grace to help us in our time of need" (Heb. 4:16). Because a disciple knows he can come boldly to God as his father, intercessory prayer has tremendous power.

Intercessory prayer clearly makes an indelible impression on God. Why are the least, the weakest in the kingdom the greatest, the strongest? Is it not because they can use the strongest weapon—intercessory prayer? God longs to be present with his people, to revive and refresh them, but he is alarmed, amazed that no one will intervene. *"He saw that there was no one, he was appalled that there was no one to intercede..."* (Isa. 59:16). God wants to bless us with his Spirit, his constant companionship and presence, but he waits to be asked. Revival, renewal, and refreshment never start with a planning committee, but with an intercessor. God is waiting for someone to kneel, fast, and pray.

---

7 William F. Arndt and F. Wilbur Gingrich, "ἀναιδεα, as, ἡ"A *Greek-English Lexicon of the New Testament and Other Early Christian Literature* (Chicago: The University of Chicago Press, 1957), 54.

Why Are We to Keep On Knocking?

"God's gonna getcha if you don't watch out," claims modern man. For many, God is a monstrous being who causes freeway accidents, brings diseases, and sends death upon people. But Jesus showed that God relates to people as a father relates to his own children.

When all of the circumstances of life seem to be going against us and the doors of life are locked, we can be certain that God cares for us. He is never too busy, far away, or inaccessible. The cries of God's people touch his heart. We can learn to depend upon him to deliver us from tribulations. In the midnights of our own personal lives, God will come to the door and give us what we need.

Jesus urges his disciples to ask of God in their prayers. We can ask of God because he is our Father and friend. The promise and guarantee of Jesus is that "everyone who asks receives." We ask because we feel a need. When we feel deep need, God is there to give us what he knows is best for us.

In the midnights of our own personal lives, God will come to the door and give us what we need.

Jesus implores us to seek God. We must seek him because we believe he's there and that he has a will for our lives. We seek because we believe he has the answer to our problems. The promise of Jesus is that "he who seeks finds." There is no doubt or hesitation on the part of

Jesus. When out of deep need we seek the will of God, we can find it.

Jesus implores us to knock, to take action. He wants us to never give up nor ever be ashamed or embarrassed to ask, but rather to be persistent and constant in our prayer life. Even though the door may be locked, the promise of Jesus is that it will be opened when we knock.

In God we have a Father, a friend, and a King who cares. The injunction of Jesus is to pray persistently to God, bringing him your personal needs—for he truly cares!

Why Persist on Our Knees?

• Perhaps the solutions are more complicated than we think.

• Perhaps the solutions will take more time than we have.

• Perhaps our persistence is for our own benefit—shaping our character.

• Perhaps there are no short cuts to holiness, only struggle.

• Perhaps God is getting us ready for huge endeavors and persistence is our homework.

• Perhaps God is waiting to give us a response more powerful than we ever dreamed—when he is asked.

Two women were sewing their husbands' pants. The first lady commented, "My husband is ready to quit the church. He says the church is dying." The second lady said, "Really? My husband says the exact opposite. He believes the church is growing, alive and well." The first lady was sewing the seat in her husband's pants; the second lady was mending the knees.

Jesus wants us on our knees. He knows that the essence of intercessory prayer is supplication. God has decided that certain matters are to be his divine will. For example, he has decided that salvation is in Christ and no other human being. However, he has left other situations outside his decrees. When we encounter those situations in which his decrees are obviously not ruling, we are to pray. Our prayers call forth what God has willed and wants to happen but will not release on earth until someone here calls for it.

> Is any one of you sick? He should call the elders of the church to pray over him and anoint him with oil in the name of the Lord. And the prayer offered in faith will make the sick person well; the Lord will raise him up .... The prayer of a righteous man is powerful and effective. Elijah was a man just like us. He prayed earnestly that it would not rain, and it did not rain on the land for three and a half years. Again, he prayed, and the heavens gave rain, and the earth produced its crops (James 5:14-18).

I don't understand all the dynamics in this intercession—calling elders, anointing with oil, etc. Yet, I agree with Oswald Chambers who wrote, "Beware of reasoning about God's Word—obey it!" Elijah calls for God's will to be done, yet God is waiting for him to ask for it. There simply is no substitute, no shortcut for intercessory prayer. Non-compliance is not an option.

Our relentless prayer life drives us daily to our knees knowing that the waiting is not worthless. Is there someone whose nature can be counted upon as being solid and firm? Is there anyone whose promise is so certain, so secure, that you can always believe it? Is there someone who doesn't seem to have a credibility problem? Is there someone who doesn't forget, fail, or cover up? The major reason that we can be persistent in our prayers is that God promises to answer our prayer. Whenever we ask, seek, or knock, we are given the promise of God that we will receive, find, and enter into blessings (Luke 11:9-10). What backs up God's promise to answer our prayers? Scripture claims that God's promises are backed up by his faithfulness. God is described as "the faithful God" (Deut. 7:9). The writer of Lamentations declares to God, "Great is your faithfulness" (3:23). Twice in 1 Corinthians Paul claims that "God is faithful" (1 Cor. 1:9; 10:13). "He who promised is faithful" (Heb. 10:23b). His faithfulness is our grounds for assurance and confidence in believing that God will answer our prayers.

He Always Opens the Door

How does God demonstrate his faithfulness in answering our prayers? God demonstrates his credibility to us by his reputation and character. Through his experiences with us, God shows that he has a faithful reputation. God promised Abraham a son, land, and a great nation, and he kept his promises (Gen. 12:1-3; 22:15-18). He renewed his promises of presents, blessings, and territory to Isaac and kept his promises (Gen. 26:1-5). David had the promise of God's covenant (2 Sam. 7:4-17; Ps. 89:3, 4, 35-37). God promised King Solomon that he would give him special guidance, and He

> *Behind each of God's promises is his unchanging and constant nature.*

did (1 Kings 3:5-14; 2 Chron. 1:7-12). In short, by keeping his personal promises, God shows that he is trustworthy.

God also demonstrates his faithfulness through the power of his great name. So awesome was the name of God that the ancient Hebrews would not even pronounce it. Variations upon the name "Jehovah" show the outstanding attributes of God's good name. The name "Jehovah-Jireh" means, "the Lord will provide" (Gen. 22:14). "Jehovah-Rophi" means that God is "the miracle leader" (Exod. 15:26). "Jehovah Shalom" means "the Lord is our peace" (Judg. 6:24). "Jehovah-Rohi" means "the Lord is my Redeemer" (Isa. 44:24). These are just a few of the many instances in the

Scripture where the very name of God shows his faithfulness, reliability, and trustworthiness.

The faithfulness of God is also demonstrated by his character. Behind each of God's promises is his unchanging and constant nature.

> Because God wanted to make the unchanging nature of his purpose very clear to the heirs of what was promised, he confirmed it with an oath. God did this so that, by two unchangeable things in which it is impossible for God to lie, we who have fled to take hold of the hope offered to us may be greatly encouraged (Hebrews 6:17-18).

And Peter claims that "the Lord is not slow in keeping his promise ..." (2 Peter 3:9). God will always answer a prayer in perfect harmony with his nature. He will always answer the door.

Jesus' great promise that God will answer our prayers calls for great faith on our part. My friend Dino Roussos tells of a Greek woman who prayed for 23 years for her husband to convert. He did! It is said that Martin Luther once was so overwhelmed by the faithfulness of God that he wrote, "I forgot God when I said, 'How can this be?'" Let us not forget God today—he's our Father. He's on the other side of the door. Knock!

Questions for Discussion

■ START TALKING

☐ With one person in your group, decide whether men or women seem more open about revealing needs and desires to other persons.

☐ Share some of your thoughts about the boundary between persistence and nagging. Why do we usually avoid the perception of nagging?

■ ENCOUNTERING THE PARABLES

☐ Some parables are difficult to bring into our culture today. Can you imagine a judge in our courts ignoring a legitimate legal complaint, as did the judge in Jesus' story? Are we more or less likely than the host in Jesus' story to knock on a neighbor's door at midnight and ask for help in accommodating a guest? Why?

☐ How astonished are you by these stories about persistent prayer? What makes these stories startling? Does God value persistent prayers? Does the depth of the need expressed in prayer make a difference to God?

☐ How can you reconcile these stories with Jesus' warning against empty repetition in the Sermon on the Mount?

■ BRINGING IT HOME

☐ What needs would cause you to be most persistent in prayer? Health concerns? Job situations? Family troubles? Our daily battle with Satan? Add to this list. Explain your thoughts and opinions.

☐ Commit with your group to a season of prayer. Encourage each other to share paramount needs with each other and the Lord. To the extent possible, place no time limit on these prayers; pray until you have adequately expressed these heartfelt concerns to God.

6

IT'S LATER
THAN YOU THINK!

I once read a story about Satan meeting with his evil spirits to plan his strategy against human beings. "Who will go to earth and persuade people to lose their souls?" he asked. The first evil spirit said, "I will go and tell them there is no heaven." A second evil spirit said, "I will go and tell them there is no hell." Then, a third spirit responded, "I will go and tell them there is no hurry." Satan told the third spirit, "Go immediately."

I would love to take you to the Milan cathedral. Look up at the 4,400 spires, turrets and steeples held up by 52 marble columns. You're gazing at Europe's third largest cathedral. But it's the window I want you to see. It stands behind the altar and is one of the largest stained glass windows in the world. Look at the scene. It's not from the ministry nor death of Jesus. It pictures the victory of Jesus Christ in a company of angels. There's Michael leading an angelic battle against the dragon. There's the magnificent angel who strides on both heaven and earth. Satan is bound with a chain and thrown in a bottomless pit for all eternity. The main image is the white horse whose rider is followed by the army of heaven. He finally comes to bring justice, peace, and final judgment. With his coming, time stops. Eternity begins.

Jesus knows he will someday ride that white horse so he stresses the urgency of accepting and following the rule of God. It has come; it is at hand; it is here. Jesus presses the urgency of obedience. With history rapidly moving toward a final moment of judgment, there is no time to lose! Seeing the sweep of God's grand design and purpose, Jesus insists that it is the last hour!

> But encourage one another daily, as long as it is called Today, so that none of you may be hardened by sin's deceitfulness (Hebrews 3:13).

> I tell you, now is the time of God's favor, now is the day of salvation (2 Corinthians 6:2b).

How late is it? Why accept Christ today? Jesus has answered these questions by way of his parables that serve to say, "It's later than you think!"

Virgins

Several of the ancient Mediterranean nations considered virgins of tremendous value to their culture, customs, and ceremonies. The vestal virgins of Rome, for instance, received special privileges for rendering service in special religious ceremonies. The story of Esther indicates that people looked upon a virgin as a candidate for royalty. Apparently, her freedom from sexual relationships allowed her complete devotion and the total commitment necessary for leadership.[1]

Young virgins traditionally served in several ceremonies, including marriage. Ancient custom spells out their place in the marriage ceremony. They would stay in a special room at a traveler's inn located near the gates of the city. There they would wait for the bridegroom and his bridal party to arrive for the wedding. The bridesmaids carried special torches (not household lamps), which were soaked in oil and handed down from one generation of family weddings to the next. Custom also said that the bridegroom and his party must arrive precisely at midnight. Usually his arrival was announced by a member of his party blowing a trumpet or calling out from the walls of the city. The bridesmaids then lit their torches and accompanied the bridegroom to the home of the bride. The wedding celebration came to a conclusion when the bridegroom went to the home of the bride and she accompanied him to his parents' house.[2] Some of these customs still

---

1   George A. Buttrick, ed., *The Interpreter's Dictionary of the Bible*, Vol. 4 (Nashville: Abingdon Press, 1962), 787-788.

2   Joachim Jeremias, *Rediscovering the Parables* (New York: Charles Scribner's Sons, 1966), 137. For additional background reading on marriage customs surrounding this parable see K.C. Pillai, *Light Through An Eastern Window* (New York: Steller and Sons, 1963), 9-14.

continue in Palestine today.

Since a torch would burn only a few minutes, thoughtful preparation included taking plenty of oil in a small jar. A bridegroom might be delayed because of necessary bargaining between his parents and hers concerning the gifts to be paid to the bride's parents. After the arrival of the bridegroom, a special wedding banquet would take place; all of those present and prepared for the wedding feast would be invited to attend. Those who procrastinated and arrived late for the wedding feast would be refused entry.

The Ten Virgins (Matt. 25:1-13)

In order to stress the urgency, the actual emergency, of the coming of the kingdom of God to a person's life, Jesus told a story.

The kingdom of heaven will be like ten virgins who were going to meet the bridegroom. Five of the bridesmaids took enough oil for their torches and no more. But the other five bridesmaids took enough oil for their torches and some in reserve. Not knowing exactly when the bridegroom and his party would come, the ten bridesmaids waited. The evening wore on into the late hours. Since the bridegroom's bargaining took longer than expected, the bridesmaids became very drowsy and fell asleep. At midnight, they were awakened with the announcement: "Here's the bridegroom!

Come out to meet him!" Then all the bridesmaids woke up and lit their torches. But five of the torches would no longer burn, for there was not enough oil. So the five bridesmaids who owned these torches said to the others, "Give us some of your oil, for our torches will not burn." "No," said the five wise virgins, "There won't be enough for all of us. You'll have to go to those who sell oil and buy from them." So the five bridesmaids went off searching for oil for their torches. While they were gone, the bridegroom arrived. The five virgins who were ready went in with him to the wedding banquet, after which the doors were closed. The celebration began, with eating, drinking, music, and dancing. Later, the other five bridesmaids arrived, pleading, "Open the door for us!" But the bridegroom replied, "I don't know you." And the door remained shut.

After Jesus finished, we can imagine him leaning forward, looking into the eyes of those around him as he said, "Therefore keep watch, because you do not know the day or the hour." To those on the outer edge of commitment to him, Jesus would stress, "See how critical it is for you to accept now the rule of God in your own lives." Jesus would press his point: "The wedding day is here! The bridegroom will arrive at any moment! Get ready for the wedding banquet! If you accept God's rule, you may attend the wedding banquet! And then the door will be shut!" Jesus urges, "It's later than you think."

A Fig Tree

The ancient world admired fig trees so much that some people considered them almost sacred. They symbolized prosperity, and their shade symbolized God's great favor. "In Hellenistic times figs were considered so important to the national economy that the Greeks made special laws to regulate their export."[3]

The fruit of the fig appears before the leaves. Therefore, the ancient Jewish law prohibited eating any fruit during the first three years of a tree's growth:

> When you enter the land and plant any kind of fruit tree, regard its fruit as forbidden. For three years you are to consider it forbidden; it must not be eaten. In the fourth year all its fruit will be holy, an offering of praise to the Lord. But in the fifth year you may eat its fruit. In this way your harvest will be increased. I am the Lord your God (Leviticus 19:23-25).

Based on this law, the barren fig tree of the parable would likely be at least six years old, since its first three years are bypassed. A barren fig tree

---

3   J.D. Douglas, ed., *The New Bible Dictionary* (Grand Rapids: William B. Eerdmans Publishing Co., 1975), 422.

would suggest lack of prosperity and lack of God's favor. Prized for its delicious and bountiful fruit, a fig tree that does not produce would be of no value and would be cut down.[4]

The Barren Fig Tree *(Luke 13:6-9)*

Here's another story Jesus told to illustrate the urgency of accepting the rule of God in one's life:

A man who planted a vineyard included in it (as often was the case) a fig tree. Now, the owner didn't look for fruit from the fig tree for the first three years. But at the end of the first three years, he expected it to produce. So, while in his vineyard one day, he looked at the fig tree. There was not one fig on the tree! The owner waited a year and again looked for fruit from the fig tree. No figs appeared. He waited yet another year and still there was no sign of the fig tree bearing fruit. The owner realized that the fig tree was using valuable nourishment that could be used for the grapes. (After all, he could have planted grapes in place of the fig tree.) So he ordered his gardener to cut it down but the gardener replied, "Sir, let me do something we normally do not do to fig trees—let me dig

---

4   For further reading on fig trees, see Alfred Edersheim, *The Life and Times of Jesus the Messiah*, Vol. 2 (Grand Rapids: William B. Eerdmans Publishing Co., 1953), 246-248; Jeremias, *Rediscovering the Parables*, 135-136.

around this one. Maybe it's not getting
enough air, water, or nourishment. I'll dig
deep and pull the earth back up on it. Let me
do something else unusual—let me fertilize
it." The owner gave him permission but
added, "if after one more year of you doing
everything you can and it still does not
produce, cut it down."

After Jesus had thus caught the attention of
those listening to him, he would say in effect,
"That's how urgent it is to accept the rule of God
in your own life!"

God keeps coming to us, giving us every
opportunity and never giving up on us. He gets
our attention and is willing to wait patiently for
us. He does the unusual, taking extraordinary
action in order that our lives might bear fruit.
But if after every opportunity, we refuse the rule
of God, we will not have another chance. Time
will end.

Now, But Not Forever

Using simple symbols familiar to his
audience, Jesus teaches a profound truth
concerning the nature of the kingdom of God.
He states that truth in simple language: "Behold,
I am coming soon" (Rev. 22:7,12). All of heaven
urges, "Come" (Rev. 22:17). Indeed, Christians
are urged to pray, "Maranatha!" or "Come, O
Lord" (1 Cor. 16:22). In God's very heart beats
mercy, grace, and loving kindness. So he allows

us every opportunity to come to the wedding banquet and to bear fruit. Whether or not we avail ourselves of his mercy is not his choice, but ours. He urges us to be in his family and to be a part of his body.

Jesus says, "It's later than you think!" The time is now; the bridegroom is coming; the owner is looking for a fruitful tree. It is urgent for us to accept God's mercy today, before time stops.

> *God knows that Christ will ride the white horse of victory and time will stop!*

What Time Is It?

Christianity stresses the importance of time. One Greek word for it is *chronos*, meaning a span of time, duration. We measure *chronos* with watches, schedules, and calendars. Contrary to popular notions, Christianity does not lay its greatest emphasis upon the future. It's not "pie in the sky" stuff. God's mercy is extended *now*, and the opportunity for a productive life is now. Our lives move closer and closer to judgment. God's mercy ought not to be misunderstood as weakness. *Chronos* reaches its fulfillment with Christ riding the great white horse. Today is what we have, so a wise person acts now. "It's later than you think!"

Another closely related Greek word, used 86 times in the New Testament for "time", is *kairos*. It means an unexpected, unique moment. Thus, Jerusalem didn't recognize the unique *kairos* when Jesus came to save her (Lk. 19:44).

It is a decisive point of faith, a leap, a specific and divinely ordained moment in accordance with the gracious nature of God himself. The more clearly a Christian sees the end, the more urgent becomes each day's opportunity to be used fully and completely. If we only see time as *chronos*, we could be overwhelmed with worry, obsessed with predictions about the coming of Christ, or become apathetic and discontented about our present lives. There are those who have become obsessed with *chronos* and given their major energies to prediction. If, however, we add *kairos* to our understanding of time, we see time as controlled by Christ. We know that he provides unique, unrepeatable moments of special opportunity and from this we take inspiration to live our daily lives with power. God is not so much interested in our predictions as in our daily actions. He wants us to see the unique opportunities for justice, compassion and mercy in the *here and now*. It is an adventure, you know. These daily moments are mysteries, quite unpredicted. So God says, "for the time (*kairos*) is at hand" (Rev.22: 10).

Beyond Our Control

For sheer drama, the scene of Paul speaking to Felix and his wife Drusilla is hard to match. Paul spoke to them about faith in Christ Jesus. As he stressed "righteousness, self-control, and the judgment to come, Felix was afraid and said, 'That's enough for now! You may leave. *When I find it convenient,* I will send for you'"(Acts 24:25). As far as we know, Felix never became a Christian. It was never convenient!

While we think we have time within our control, Jesus says, "It's later than you think!" How tempting it is to think that life itself is under control since we've been able to control so much of our lives. We've conquered many diseases and space, communicated across the earth, and built large arsenals of nuclear weapons—all of which may lead to a false sense of security. But we cannot control time; it's beyond our control.

Only God controls time. "No one knows about that day or hour, not even the angels in heaven, nor the Son, but only the Father" (Matt. 24:36). Jesus stresses over and over the urgency of accepting the rule of God today: "Therefore keep watch, because you do not know on what day your Lord will come... So you also must be ready, because the Son of Man will come at an hour when you do not expect him" (Matt 24:42, 44). "It's later than you think!"

I'll Do It Tomorrow

Why do we procrastinate? Why do we delay? Why do we depend upon tomorrow?

Perhaps a part of the answer is found in what happens to us. Most of our lives are spent in endeavors that allow a second chance. Ours is the society that invented erasers and correction fluid. We usually get a second chance, another opportunity to correct, improve, or try again.

Frankly it's very tempting to think that we will always get a second chance. But when it comes to God's reign in our lives, we are advised to not put confidence in "tomorrow," not to plan on further opportunities:

> Now listen, you who say, "Today or tomorrow we will go to this or that city, spend a year there, carry on business and make money." Why, you do not even know what will happen tomorrow. What is your life? You are a mist that appears for a little while and then vanishes. Instead, you ought to say, "If it is the Lord's will, we will live and do this or that" (James 4:13-15).

Jesus never says, "There's plenty of time!" He calls us to act; he places no premium on caution. Satan says, "No hurry. Do it tomorrow!" Jesus knows that when the last day of repentance passes, it is too late. One who lets God rule his life seizes the opportunity.

... in Greek mythology, 'opportunity' is pictured as a beautiful maiden who passed by a person's life only once.

In Greek mythology opportunity is pictured as a beautiful maiden who passes by a person's life only once. The Greeks picture her having long hair, flowing down the front of her face and body. As she passes by, one must seize opportunity, for she has no hair flowing down her back. There will not be a second chance.

Realizing the folly of waiting until tomorrow, Jesus possesses an unequivocal spirit about obeying God. There is no middle ground, no tomorrow, nor time to count as ours. There's no time to lose, for time belongs to God. Thus, Jesus worked to the point of exhaustion day and night to bring people to God's rule. John Bright stresses the urgency of Jesus in his fine book, *The Kingdom of God*:

> Christ, then, has come to call men to his Kingdom. His mission was not to instruct men in a better and more spiritual ethic, to impart to men a clearer understanding of the character of God, to attack those abuses which had made the Jewish law the stultification of the religious spirit and to suggest certain emendations to that law—in short, to point men the way to be better men. All this he did, indeed, and with a vengeance. But he did it in the dazzling light of the coming Kingdom. His was a call of tremendous urgency, a call of radical decision for that Kingdom. The Kingdom is *right there*, "at hand." It stands at the door and knocks (Luke 12:36, cf. Rev. 3:20). Who will open and let it in? Who will say *Yes* to its coming?[5]

---

5   John Bright, *The Kingdom of God* (Nashville: Abingdon Press, 1953), 219.

Why such urgency? Remember the coming of the white horse. "It's later than you think!"

Questions for Discussion

■ START TALKING

☐ In America, arriving at 7:30 for a 7:00 appointment would be seen as inconsiderate. Are there places in the world with a different view of punctuality than the United States? If anyone has traveled abroad and experienced this, share your observations with the group.

☐ What are the pros and cons of being punctual?

■ ENCOUNTERING THE PARABLES

☐ Why do you think Jesus told these two stories to his followers? Which of his hearers might have been astonished to think of themselves as uprooted fig trees or guests refused entry to a wedding feast?

☐ As pointed out in the last chapter, these two parables are not an isolated teaching. The entire New Testament picks up the theme of these two stories in non-story form (the epistles and Revelation). How does the urgency of this theme impact your life? Your priorities? Your relationships?

■ BRINGING IT HOME

☐ What factors in our lives, our jobs, our families, or our personalities influence us to place a lower priority on spiritual formation?

☐ What helps you avoid procrastinating in your walk with Jesus Christ? What has helped you actualize these parables?

7

THERE'S
A NEW DAY COMING

For all too many people today, life seems brutal, lonely, and meaningless. Millions have agreed with Ernest Hemingway that an early death should be considered a choice blessing. In his classic novel, *A Farewell To Arms*, Hemingway wrote, "The world breaks everyone ... Those that will not break it kills. It kills the very good and the very gentle and the very brave impartially. If you are none of these you may be sure that it will kill you too, but there will be no special hurry."[1] Fortunate is the person, according to Hemingway, who does not have to live life and discover its brutality, guilt, and loneliness.[2]

But is there ever a chance for a new beginning in life? How about a fresh start? Can there be a new day? Is there ever a time when the sun dispels the darkness of loneliness, fear, guilt, and hurt? Is there any other choice between

---

1   Ernest Hemingway, *A Farewell To Arms* (New York: Scribner, 1940), 249.

2   Carlos Baker, *Ernest Hemingway: A Life Story* (New York: Scribner, 1969), 271.

being broken by life or an early death? Is life totally absurd, or can it have purpose, direction, and meaning?

For the Christian, Jesus steps in at the point of these questions and offers God's way for a person's life. He assures us that we can find the divine authority by which to guide our lives. Through Christ, we can find the knowledge and the spiritual power to fill the blankness inside us. Jesus offers us God's rule for life in the place of self-rule. Making God's rule possible was the central purpose in Jesus' earthly life.

> The Spirit of the Lord is on me, because he has anointed me to preach good news to the poor. He has sent me to proclaim freedom for the prisoners and recovery of sight for the blind, to release the oppressed, to proclaim the year of the Lord's favor (Luke 4:18-19).

Jesus offered another option to a hopeless and lonely world. He made a grand announcement in the symbolic language of parables. Through word pictures of fig trees, wineskins, and banquets, Jesus made his declaration: "There's a new day coming!"

Fig Trees (Matt. 24:32-35; Mark 18:28-32; Luke 21:29-33)

As mentioned in the last chapter, ancient people considered fig trees symbols of prosperity, peace, and triumph. In Latin mythology, Bacchus held the fig tree sacred and it was employed in numerous religious ceremonies. The Romans considered the fig tree their chief symbol for the future prosperity of Rome.

The Old Testament frequently refers to the fig tree. Jews regarded figs "so valuable, that to cut them down if they yielded even a small measure of fruit was popularly deemed to deserve death at the hand of God."[3] Ancient Israel considered figs a special attraction in the promised land, which they described as "a land of wheat and barley, vines and fig trees, pomegranates…" (Deut. 8:8). In order to show the great prosperity of Palestine, the spies brought back figs (Num. 13:23). When Israel wanted to describe the desolation and poverty of the wilderness, they described it as a place with "no grain or figs, grapevines or pomegranates…" (Num. 20:5). To show the future prosperity of Israel, the prophet Joel used the fig tree as an emblem when he wrote "… for the open pastures are becoming green. The trees are bearing their fruit; the fig tree and the vine yield their riches" (Joel 2:22). "Almost all the references to the fruit

---

3   Alfred Edersheim, *The Life and Times of Jesus The Messiah*, Vol. 2 (Grand Rapids: William B. Eerdmans Publishing Co., 1953), 246.

of the fig tree," writes one interpreter, "are indications of its great importance to the life of ancient times, as it continues to be in the Holy Land today."[4]

Before fig trees yielded a bumper crop, they required years of patient care. This passage of time is integral to our understanding of the parable of Luke 13:6-9. Jews regarded the fig tree as the most fruitful of all trees. They gave it the favored place in the vineyard.[5] Even today, the fig trees of the Holy Land remain bare until the beginning of spring. Then a remarkable process takes place. Unlike many of the other trees of Palestine, just when the fig tree's bare branches appear to be dead, it begins to put out small leaf buds and, at the same time, tiny figs begin to appear in the leaf axils. These early signs of spring herald new life, a new time of the year.[6]

The Budding Fig Tree
(Matt. 24:32-35; Mark 13:28-32; Luke 21:29-33)

Jesus declared in each of these parables that the time had come for the rule of God in the hearts and lives of people. The prophets had

---

4 J.C. Thever, "Fig Tree," *The Interpreter's Dictionary of the Bible*, Vol. 2 (Nashville: Abingdon Press, 1962), 267.

5 Edersheim, op. cit., 247.

6 For further background on fig trees, read E. W. Masterman, "Fig, Fig-Tree," *International Standard Bible Encyclopedia*, Vol. 2, 1108-1109; Joachim Jeremias, *Rediscovering the Parables* (New York: Charles Scribner's Sons, 1966), 93-94.

yearned for this long-awaited new day and had predicted its coming. But when will this new day arrive? To some students of the Bible, the context in which this parable was told seems to point to the second coming of Christ. But others believe that these parables point to the coming of the kingdom of God. Thus, Jesus would be announcing the new day of the rule of God, the day of salvation. And he does so by saying once more, "Let me tell you a story."

Throughout the winter, the fig tree sheds all its leaves, remains bare, and gives every appearance of deadness. But have you noticed that as winter turns to spring, its twigs become tender and it puts out delicate, green leaves? Even though it appears to have been dead, the fig tree now gives every evidence of life. Winter is over, and summer is near.

Then, Jesus turned to his disciples and his enemies and said, in effect, "That's the way the rule of God can be in a person's life. It is near." Evidences of deadness appear in every person's life: guilt, loneliness, confusion, meaninglessness, and insensitivity to others. But Jesus announced that a new day was coming! The winter of the old covenant now gives way to the summer of God's new covenant. The rule of God in the lives of individuals is close at hand! Jesus has come! There is hope!

Garments and Wine
(Matt. 9:16-17; Mark 2:21-22; Luke 5:36-38)

It was a necessity for the poor to repair a worn robe, since buying a new one was out of the question. In order to repair a torn old garment, cloth needed to be "dressed," or shrunk to prevent further tearing. It is possible that Jesus may have watched his mother mend threadbare garments using this exact technique.[7]

The reference "new wine" referred to wine made "from the first drippings of the juice before the winepress was trodden. As such it would be particularly potent."[8] Jews placed new wine in a new goatskin pouch (Josh. 9:4, 13). A new leather pouch would be pliable and flexible enough to expand with the fermenting new wine. But new wine in a cracked, hard, old wineskin would burst the skin. New wine required a fresh wineskin.

New Garment, New Wineskin
(Matt. 9:16-17; Mark 2:21-22; Luke 5:36-38)

When Jesus was challenged by John's disciples as to why his disciples did not fast, he heard a deeper question: a challenge to his

---

7 George A. Buttrick, *The Parables of Jesus* (New York: Harper & Brothers, 1928), 6.

8 F. S. Fitzsimmonds, "Wine and Strong Drink," *The New Bible Dictionary* (Grand Rapids: William B. Eerdmans Publishing Co., 1975), 1331.

authority to announce a new day. Perhaps change frightened his questioners, or maybe they had become comfortable in their traditions. In responding to the challenge, Jesus told his hearers a story.

You know how a woman patches an old garment. She does not take a new patch and sew it on an old garment. If she did, there would be shrinking and tearing.

You have seen how men pour new wine into wineskins. They put the new wine in a new wineskin so that when the fermentation begins the wineskin will expand. If they place the new wine in a stretched, cracked, and old wineskin, it would burst. The wine and wineskin would be lost.

Then, Jesus turned to his inquirers and said, in effect, "That's the way it is with the kingdom of God. There's a new day coming!" The old garment and the old wineskin may point to either worn-out Judaism with its threadbare forms and traditions or to a person's hardened, inflexible heart. The new garment and the new wine signal a new day, a fresh direction for the lives of people. Jesus invited everyone to wear the new garment! All are invited to drink the new wine! Here, then, is the heart of the good news: "Therefore, if anyone is in Christ, he is a new creation; the old has gone, the new has come!" (2 Cor. 5:17).

The God Who Acts

The Old Testament is filled with hope of a coming new day. Some seven hundred and fifty years before Jesus spoke the parables Isaiah described it:

> "Then will the eyes of the blind be opened and the ears of the deaf unstopped. Then will the lame leap like a deer, and the tongue of the dumb shout for joy. Water will gush forth in the wilderness and streams in the desert. The burning sand will become a pool, the thirsty ground bubbling springs" (Isaiah 35:5-7a).

The prophetic word is but one Old Testament tributary constantly flowing into the larger stream of the kingdom of God. The belief and hope that God would act in history, that a new day was coming, and that a Messianic age was in the future had their origins in the headwaters of the covenant with Abraham (Gen. 12:1-3). The Mosaic covenant and the beliefs of the nation of Israel continued to feed the stream of hope that God would act in history. Later, in the years of captivity and religious apostasy, the stream would be reduced to only a small trickle in the parched desert.

On the pages of the New Testament, the stream of hope and expectation becomes a mighty, rushing torrent. "But when the time had fully come, God sent his Son..." (Gal. 4:4). The New Testament centers in the new, here-and-now activity of God. "For God so loved the world that he gave his one and only Son..." (John 3:16). The New Testament should not be thought of as a book about some new ethic, new religion, or new view of God and man. As John Bright has pointed out, "Jesus did not announce to the Jews that a loftier notion of God was now available—but that their God had acted!"[9] This does not undercut the supremacy of the New Testament to the Old, but it is a mistake to set the New Testament *against* the Old. The New Testament declares that the God of creation and history "became flesh and lived for a little while among us" (John 1:14). God, whose activity was longed for, hoped for, and prayed for, has acted decisively in Jesus Christ. This is the message of these parables. At last, the summer of God's salvation is here. His long-awaited banquet is now being served. It is time to put on the new garments and get on with the celebration!

'Follow Me'

The New Testament heralds the coming of Jesus of Nazareth to be the grand, climactic activity of God. Before the coming of Jesus, the kingdom of God was described in future tense. Jesus changed the tense of the rule of God to the present. For example, early in his Galilean

---

9 John Bright, *The Kingdom of God* (Nashville: Abingdon Press, 1953), 195.

ministry, Jesus announced a new day: "The time has come. The kingdom of God is near. Repent and believe the good news!" (Mark 1:15). Immediately, Jesus began to call men to him in order that God might rule their hearts.

Some who answered the call of Jesus, however, misread him. They looked for a political kingdom, a government more powerful than Rome that would be able to rule the world by Jesus' leadership. Even as Jesus spoke of "the kingdom of God," they cast his ideas in political terms. Consequently, many misunderstood the nature of God's rule. It would be easy to do—almost natural, given the Jews' history.

Jesus changed the tense of the rule of God to the present.

Imagine yourself as a Jew living in a small Galilean village in A.D. 30. The old men tell of past glories—days of King David's rule over the Mediterranean basin a thousand years ago. Israel was not only the most powerful nation, she was God's chosen nation. Under Solomon, she rose to become the envy of her neighbors. They came from all over the world to view her greatness. But the old men continued their story by telling of her fall, her domination by Assyrians, Babylonians, Persians, Greeks, Syrians, and now Romans. The old men cried as their hearts broke, their hope flickered, and their passion ebbed. Some would recall the promise of the future: *"A great leader will one day lead Israel back to glory."* Numerous Jews rose on the horizon and laid claim to Messiahship: Judas, son of Hezekiah,

Simon, who lead a revolt in Perea, Athronges of Judea—a shepherd who led an attack against the Roman army—Theudas, and others. Each said, "Follow me." Each promised to restore Israel to the glory days of David. Each was repressed and conquered.

Now a carpenter from Nazareth appears in A.D. 30 saying, "Follow me." Given Jewish history and a background of hope, no wonder Peter, Andrew, James, and John immediately "left their nets and followed him" (Mark 1:19-20). Jesus takes the apostles right where he finds them—with political and personal agendas, confused and searching, and with questionable motives. Perhaps, as they listen to his stories and watch his life, they will understand the new day coming upon them. Maybe they'll even understand it's not political! Even his enemies misunderstood Jesus' heavenly agenda.

As they increased their opposition toward Jesus, they understood less and less of his parables. He began to reserve the deep meaning of his parables for those who already had committed themselves to him. Even today, if we try to understand the kingdom of God in any sense other than the one he gave us, then we, too, will miss the deep meaning! God isn't anxious to rule over the earth. "The kingdom of God does not come visibly" (Luke 17:20). But he is wanting very much to rule the hearts of all people. So, we should pray, "Your kingdom come" (Matt.6:10). What is required is openness of heart and humility of spirit. With this beginning, our understanding of the rule of God and its special nature becomes clear and evident.

And by the way... he'll take you right where he finds you. Even when you misunderstand kingdom business, he'll stay with you.

Inside Job

If you have experienced guilt, loneliness, confusion, and fear, join the human race. None of us can live without personal worth, security, affirmation, and love. Yet, unless God has acted on our behalf, life becomes a random collection of happenings. Ugliness and meaninglessness become the norm. Our choices narrow down to two: a life with no hope—or death. Like Camus, we feel that life has "No Exit." We feel totally controlled by circumstances.

God does not seek to 'scotch-tape' blessings to my life but stands ready to completely fill my life, inside out.

God's word rings out really good news: "There's a new day coming." A new thing has happened—God has acted! And he has acted for you and me. He wants to bring meaning to my life. God doesn't seek to "scotch-tape" blessings to my life, but stands ready to completely fill my life, inside out. "Here I am! I stand at the door and knock. If anyone hears my voice and opens the door, I will go in and eat with him, and he with me" (Rev. 3:20).

Here at thy table, Lord / This sacred
    hour;
O. let us feel Thee near / In loving
    pow'r;
Calling our thoughts away / From self
    and sin,
As to thy banquet hall / We enter in.

Sit at the feast, dear Lord / Break Thou
    the bread;
Fill Thou the cup that brings / Life to
    the dead;
That we may find in Thee / Pardon and
    peace;
And from all bondage win / A full
    release.

So shall our life of faith / Be full, be
    sweet;
And we shall find our strength / For
    each day meet:
Fed by Thy living bread / All hunger
    past,
We shall be satisfied / And saved at last.

Come then, O Holy Christ / Feed us,
    we pray;
Touch with Thy pierced hand / Each
    common day;
Making this earthly life / Full of Thy
    grace,
Till in the home of heav'n / We find our
    place.

           – William E. Sherwin

Thank God! A new day has come!

Questions for Discussion

■ START TALKING

☐ What's your favorite time of day? Let each member share reasons for his or her choice.

☐ If you've overcome a bad or annoying habit like being late, forgetting names, running out of gas, or whatever, share your breakthrough and how it felt to experience such a transformation.

■ ENCOUNTERING THE PARABLES

☐ Each parable in this chapter tells of a new beginning with God's rule in our lives. Since Herod and Rome dominated Israel in Jesus' time, why might these stories astonish persons of that day who lived in Jerusalem? Are these stories less astonishing to us today? Why or why not?

☐ Even though the Old Testament anticipates God's new day, it was not easy for some people to connect Jesus with these expectations. In your opinion, what kept Jesus' hearers from making the connection? What keeps people in our time from connecting Jesus with God's new day, his rule in their lives?

■ BRINGING IT HOME

☐ What barriers keep us from accepting the rule of God in our hearts and lives today: Skepticism? Fear? Inconvenience? Ambivalence? Name any other possibilities that come to mind.

☐ What steps do we need to take to accept God more fully as king of our lives? How can members of this group help each other in this process?

8

A Terrorist, A Prostitute, and a Few Church Members

How would you start a great religious movement? I mean one that would change the world; one that would champion the value of people; one that would promise the grace of God. One that would offer heaven. Well, if you offer big things you're going to need—

Big money.

A big city... Good location... Important people who are well-connected... Lots of promotion, packaging, marketing, and endorsements... Frequent sound bites and well-placed press releases... Appearances from Hollywood, New York City—maybe even the White House!

Now, that's the way to start a successful movement! At least, that's the way we would do it.

Maybe there's another way. Suppose you started with a truck driver from New Jersey, a Paris prostitute, a former convicted felon, an Oxford professor, and a taxi driver from Brasilia. You have no money, no media coverage, and no

big city from which to launch the movement—
only a few people whose beliefs and lives will
form its foundation.

Ridiculous? Maybe so, but what if such
humble materials could be transformed into an
unbelievably powerful social force? What if the
success of this movement is measured by how
one person lives? What if the benchmark of a
movement has to do more with sacrifice than
success? What if the real gauge of a movement is
how it ends, not simply how it's launched?

For just a moment, think differently. You
start in a small, troubled country which nobody's
ever heard of, with no money, and no
advertising. You have four fisherman, several tax
collectors, a terrorist, a few prostitutes and a
handful of average people who bring very little to
the table. You talk about *raw* material! Almost
any adviser would tell you that you just planned
your next mistake!

Before you lay this idea aside, let Jesus tell
you a few stories. Stories that reveal a
fundamental truth about the rule of God in the
lives of people. To really appreciate and
understand this truth means to look beyond what
you see and to listen for more than you hear.

> This is why I speak to them in
> parables: though seeing, they do not
> see; though hearing, they do not hear
> or understand. In them is fulfilled the
> prophecy of Isaiah: You will ever be
> hearing but never understanding;

You will be ever seeing but never perceiving (Matthew 13:13-14).

As you listen to his stories, you'll be simply astonished—they don't seem logical!

Mustard Seeds and Leaven

Before listening to his stories about mustard seeds and leaven, Jesus would want us to have some understanding as to why he is talking about such things. You see, Jewish rabbis use the phrase "small as a mustard seed" as a proverb to refer to the very smallest amount, remnant, or residue.[1] So, our Lord's phrase "faith as small as a mustard seed" communicates clearly to the people of his day the tiniest germ of faith.

In biblical times, several types of mustard had extraordinarily tiny seeds. Perhaps you've seen necklaces and other pieces of jewelry made with mustard seeds. As one writer explains, "the seeds of the East are really about one-tenth of the size of the ones that grow in America and Europe. They are truly the smallest of seeds, and the plants that they produce grow as large as trees."[2] The pinhead size of a mustard seed, "...the smallest seed you plant in the ground"

1   Alfred Edersheim, *The Life and Times of Jesus the Messiah*, (Grand Rapids: William B. Eerdmans Publishing Co., 1953), Vol. 1, 593.

2   K.C. Pillai, *Light Through An Eastern Window* (New York: Speller and Sons, 1963), 100.

(Mark 4:31), distinguishes it from other Palestinian seeds. Under favorable conditions, a mustard seed might grow into a very tall shrub or tree, reaching ten to twelve feet in height. " ...It grows and becomes the largest of all garden plants, with such big branches that the birds of the air can perch in its shade" (Mark 4:32).

Bread is the most important part of the Middle Eastern diet. If you have no bread, you have no meal! Whatever else is prepared only supplements the bread. So, bread making is an ancient and necessary art. It's a relatively simple process.

A Middle Eastern woman mixes flour with water and salt in a special trough. To bake leavened bread, she adds a piece of dough "retained from a former baking, which had fermented and turned acid[ic]."[3] Then she either dissolves the leaven in water before adding flour or she adds the leaven to the flour and continues to mix. According to custom, she covers the dough with a cloth and leaves it to stand overnight. By morning, the yeast has penetrated the entire loaf. Its lively chemical action dynamically moves through the bread. No noise! No attention given! Quiet penetration! She completes the process by baking the bread over hot stones or in an oven.

What does "leaven" symbolize? On the one hand, Scripture describes leaven as a symbol of corruption. It has the capacity to spread its

3   J.D. Douglas, "Leaven," *The New Bible Dictionary* (Grand Rapids: William B. Eerdmans Pulishing Co., 1975), 275.

fermenting power. Jesus warns against the hypocrisy of the Pharisees and the Sadducees (Matthew 16:11). In the same way, Paul holds up the yellow flag against a little moral corruption, which might throw an entire church into moral confusion (1 Cor. 5:6-8). "A little yeast works through the whole batch of dough" (Galatians 5:9).

However, leaven also stands for the positive process of moral influence. When Jesus likens the growth of the kingdom of God among people to the pervasive working of the yeast, he uses leaven as a symbol for spiritual development.

The Mustard Seed and the Leaven
(Matthew 13:31-33; Luke 13:18-21)

Lonely. Curious. Guilty. Unknown. Lost in the crowd. Gathered around the storyteller. Listening…

Let me tell you a story about the tiniest of all seeds, a mustard seed. One day, a man planted it in his field. Days turned into weeks and weeks into months. Guess what happened?

The man found that this tiny seed had grown into a huge mustard tree with birds in its branches.

Then Jesus turns to the crowd and says, in effect, "that's the way the rule of God works in the life of a person."

It's a tiny beginning and easily overlooked. It doesn't draw attention to itself. It's quiet. Personal. God begins with someone in the crowd, someone with an open heart and life. You would never imagine it. God's rule moves from person to person. Its origin is so small; its end is so great! From totally lost to godliness. From a nobody to a somebody.

Even God's rule among nations starts with a common people in a despised land. But his rule moves among the ethnic groups of the earth. It includes men and women, Jews and Gentiles, all races, all languages, and all nations. What a magnificent contrast: from a tiny beginning to the greatest ending! Guilty, lonely, hurting people become God's redeemed for all ages.

After speaking about a mustard seed, Jesus looks into the faces of the crowd and tells them another story:

You know how a woman bakes bread. Before going to bed at night, she takes time to gather all the necessary ingredients. Well, one night, a woman planned to make enough bread to feed more than a hundred people. She took a scrap of leaven and placed it into a bushel of dough. Because it was such a large amount, she mixed the dough until she worked it throughout the batch. She covered the dough with a cloth and went to sleep. Guess what happened while she was asleep? All through the night, the yeast had worked its way through the bread. By morning, the

dough had swollen and become much larger due to the quiet work of the yeast. Now she was ready to bake it on hot stones and serve it in the village.

Then, Jesus would again say, in essence, "that's the way the rule of God works in your life." Like yeast, it begins with a tiny, quiet, almost unnoticeable beginning. When the rule of God comes into your life, it also starts to work at once—quietly, powerfully, gradually.

A sure signal that God is at work is his boundless vitality. He permeates your values, purposes, career, and relationships. Such a radical change may bring intimidation, curiosity, apathy, and even persecution. But one thing is always true of the growth of God's rule: nothing can stop it! It's quiet. Tiny. But the beginning of something great!

Seed Time to Harvest

How can the infinitely great be contained in the infinitely small?

Well, Jesus uses images from farming, including planting and harvesting. Every Palestinian farm family is familiar with the cycle. Seed time for ancient Palestinian farmers usually fell in late November or December. A farmer might either sow seed by plowing it under the ground or plow the ground first and then sow the seed. In either case, a farmer would broadcast the seed across the soil. At times, a farmer might use cattle to tread the seed into the soil.

> In the latter case, a sack with holes was filled with corn and laid on the back of the animal, so that, as it moved onwards, the seed was thickly scattered. Thus it might well be, that it would fall indiscriminately on beaten roadway, on stony places but thinly covered with soil, or where the thorns had not been cleared away, or undergrowth from the thorn-hedge crept into the field, as well as on good ground.[4]

In the Old Testament, proper farming employed only fertile, rich soil (Job 5:6; Proverbs 24:30-32). Any other kind of soil was considered non-productive. Of course, the productivity of any crop depended in great measure on rainfall. Heavy winter rains usually gave the crops enough moisture, but the rains of March and April were needed to bring the grain harvest.

Harvest marked the end of the growing season, a time for gathering in the fruits of labor. This usually fell during the middle of April, following the spring rains. Old Testament references described how the harvest began with the barley and ended with the wheat. This harvest ended with the feast of Passover (Lev. 23:9-14; 2 Samuel 21:9-10). The most thorough

---

4   Edersheim, op. cit., Vol. 1, 586-587.

Old Testament description of harvest is found in Ruth 2 and 3. Workers collected the sheaves into a heap and removed them to threshing floors. Unmuzzled oxen trod upon the grain, separating the chaff and the straw from the grain. By use of a fan and with the help of the wind, a harvester would winnow the grain. The remaining grain would be placed in storage bins.[5]

Palestinian farmers considered a ten percent increase in the seed sown to be a good harvest. In comparison, thirty, sixty, and a hundred percent symbolized an unusual bounty.[6]

The Sower
(Matthew 13:3-8; Mark 4:3-8; Luke 8:5-8)

What a strange pulpit: a boat! But what a sermon!

Jesus crawled into a boat one day to tell one of his stories, a tale that would make every farmer burst with pride.

All of you farmers will appreciate this story. One day, a farmer prepared his field and began to sow seed. Some of the seed fell where the birds could eat it. Other seed fell on the path alongside the field, where the sun could scorch it. Some seed even fell among

---

5   John M'Clintock and James Strong, "Harvest," *Cyclopaedia of Biblical, Theological and Ecclesiastical Literature*, Vol. 4 (New York: Harper and Brothers, 1891), 93-94.

6   Archibald Hunter, *Interpreting the Parables* (Philadelphia: the Westminster Press, 1960), 47; Jeremias, *Rediscovering the Parables*, 119.

rocks and thorns. Guess what happened to some of the other seed? It fell into rich, fertile, prepared earth. The rest is almost unbelievable!

After months of patient waiting and refreshing rain, the small seed began to produce a huge crop. The bounty was unusually large! Can you believe that the harvest turned out to be thirty times larger than the seed? Some was fifty times larger than the seed and some even a hundred times larger. All were amazed at the harvest!

Then Jesus explained to the crowds, "that's the way God works in the hearts and lives of people. Even the tiniest seed which God plants produces an unbelievable harvest!"

I'm sure you've noticed that sometimes the ways of God are quiet, still, and not very dramatic. In a world that looks for every great event to be accompanied by sound and fury, the rule of God in the life of people may seem too quiet to take seriously. It's just a handful of seeds! But God nourishes those seeds and in his own time, he brings about a harvest that surpasses all human expectations and measures. It's a tiny beginning, but take care—don't overlook it!

A Patient Farmer (Mark 4:26-29)

When will this happen? I mean, if you're interested in the bottom line and if time is money, how long is this going to take? If you're out to change the world, you can't be all day about it! Is it today? If not, why bother?

These are the kinds of questions that haunted men like Peter, John, Simon the Zealot, and Judas. Can Rome be overthrown? Hope flickered. Even though some had given up, others remembered the promise: "One day a great leader will return and restore the kingdom to the glory of David. He'll crush our enemies. He will unify our nation. We must have the Messiah. What counts is the kingdom. It must be restored at all costs."

At this point, Jesus steps into the picture. "Follow me," he says. Should we assume that when his first disciples heard him say this, they automatically thought, "This is the Son of God! We're going to establish the Church. We're going to write the New Testament. We're going to teach our people to love their enemies"?

No, when Peter, Andrew, James, and John dropped their nets and followed him, it may not have been entirely for the right reasons. Even though their political motives were self-serving, Jesus still allowed them to follow. He knew that the rule of God in their lives would take time.

With remarkable patience, Jesus turns the human race around, one person at a time. Maybe that's why he spent so much of his time with twelve men. He could have infused in them miraculous, instant understanding, instant commitment, and instant maturity. He could have... but he didn't.

Instead he told them this story:

Watch a farmer broadcast seed. As he throws the seed on fertile land, it grows both during the night and day. Whether the farmer wakes up in the night to check his crop or whether he sleeps through the night, the seed continues to grow. Day after day, his crop slowly matures. He's patient with the crop. He watches the seed spontaneously producing the stalk, then the head, and then the full kernel that's ready for harvest. When the harvest time comes, the happy farmer cuts down his crop. Even as he takes in his harvest, he doesn't fully understand how a small seed sprouted into a full kernel. He just had to wait patiently.

Again, Jesus turns to his disciples in the hope that they will get the point: God works on his own agenda in bringing his rule into the lives of people. Regardless of circumstances or conditions, God's seed quietly grows toward harvest. Turning it into a political or military mission in order to speed the process only plays into the hands of God's enemy. Wait patiently for God. It takes time to turn terrorists, prostitutes, and even churchgoers into God's people.

How long will it take? Only God can answer that. In faith, God's people join him in his mission and believe with confidence and assurance that he will bring his mission to full accomplishment.

Tiny Beginnings and Triumphant Ends

We live in a noisy world! Notice that the TV ads have an increased volume level to get your attention. People today suffer from the activist delusion that nothing significant happens unless it's accompanied by a loud noise. We're tempted to believe that noise and news go together. According to the best marketing procedures, any new thing must be accompanied by neon lights, fireworks, and spotlights.

How different is the work of God! Quiet. Unnoticeable. Never drawing attention to itself for the sake of attention!

If you doubt that, recall for a moment that God's own son was born in a manger. Not in Rome, not in Caesar's household, not in a palace, not to the announcement of trumpets, not even in the Bethlehem Hilton. Such simplicity bothers some people who have difficulty in realizing that God is at home with a humble address.

It's tempting to think that if we could change the routine of our daily lives, God would be more real to us. But Jesus astonishes us with his stories. God works through the ordinary details of daily life. The power of his Holy Spirit turns an average Thursday into a day of triumph. So if we only look for God in religious settings and on religious days, we will miss many of the quiet, tiny, yet highly significant works of Christ in our lives—even as some missed his birth.

After the birth of Jesus, who would have dreamed that a carpenter's son would herald a new day of God? Such a tiny beginning even confused his own family, his own disciples.

> The Kingdom of God, then, is a power already released in the world. True, its beginnings are tiny, and it might seem incredible that the humble ministry of this obscured Galilean could be the dawning of a new age of God. Yet it is! What has been begun here will surely go on to its conclusion; nothing can stop it. And the conclusion is victory.[7]

Think about those that Jesus called to be his disciples! These first-century Jews saw Jesus as the long-awaited political Messiah. Their political longing had existed much too long. They were ready to move out of Galilee in force against Rome's Tenth Legion, stationed at Caesarea. They were ready to fight.

Their expectations were so strong that they struggled with Jesus and his understanding of the kingdom of God. "Jesus spoke the word to them, as much as they could understand" (Mark 4:33). The first time Jesus announced that he was going to die, Peter struggled, fought with such an idea, and argued with Jesus, as if to say, "You are *not* going to die. That's not the way this works" (Mark 8:31-32).

The apostles? No credentials, small in number, little education, no money, and no

---

7   John Bright, *The Kingdom of God* (Nashville: Abingdon Press, 1953), 218.

contacts in Rome. Add to this that they just seemed to miss the point about the business of the kingdom. Even after being with Jesus for a long time, they still didn't understand. They struggled with him and he struggled with them:

- Don't you understand? (Mark 4:13)

- Are you so dull, don't you see? (Mark 7:17)

- Do you still not see or understand? (Mark 8:17)

- Do you still not understand? (Mark 8:21)

Who would have ever dreamed that this small group of unknown men would spread the Christian faith through the first century world?

Look at the way God began his church! It had a tiny beginning—easily overlooked or considered an insignificant event in history. The Romans would not have placed the events of Acts 2 in the Top Ten News Events of the Year. But God works through insignificant beginnings to bring triumph. His church has endured. Rome fell!

Great in the Small

Suppose the same spiritual principle that God uses might work in your own life? For instance, when you pray nightly with your children, that may seem like the tiniest of events. Or when you get your family together on family night and study the Bible, pray, and talk about God, it may seem an insignificant moment. But... suppose it is one of God's ways of raising up future leaders of his church. Teaching a group of children every Sunday morning may seem like an unnoticed event. But this could be one of God's ways of developing committed missionaries, dedicated husbands and wives, and strong single people. Prayer and fasting are done in secret. But they elevate us to a new spiritual plane.

So, God calls his people to give a "cup of cold water in his name," to encourage the widow, to care for the homeless children—small events capable of triumphant ends. Who would have ever dreamed that an encouraging word given to a prisoner or a sick person might ultimately lead them to Christ? No wonder that on the Day of Judgment, God places such heavy stress on small acts of service.

He calls upon his church to see the validity of the way he works: the infinitely great can be seen in the infinitely small.

The dramatic can arise from the not so dramatic. Life springs from death. Washing feet brings glory. For the people of God, success is measured by God's standards, not any other.

A Quiet, Prevailing Force

Nothing can stop the rule of God!

His timing mystifies us. We want things done quickly. But an unwavering patience is essential if we are to see the work of God in today's world. The planted seed will bring forth fruit in due season. Despite all the appearances to the contrary, God is at work in our world. Never doubt it!

Doubt is nothing new to God; he has seen it before. When Pliny the Younger (62-113 A.D.) wrote to the Roman emperor, Trajan, he described Rome's efforts to stop Christianity:

> The matter seems to me to justify my consulting you, especially on account of the number of those in peril; for many persons of all ages and classes and of both sexes are being put in peril by accusations [that they are Christians], and this will go on. The contagion of this superstition has spread not only in the cities, but in the villages and rural districts as well; yet it seems capable of being checked and set right.[8]

Pliny the Younger overlooked one thing... God!

---

8 For the entire letter, see Henry Bettenson, ed., *Documents of the Christian Church* (New York: Oxford University Press, 1967), 3-4.

Questions for Discussion

▮ START TALKING

☐ Find a partner and share some guesses about why God launched his kingdom as he did.

☐ Why do you suppose God began with a carpenter's son from Nazareth, eleven Galileans, and a Judean treasurer named Judas, instead of a Roman senator backed by the Roman military?

☐ If Jesus came today, would he be accompanied by a media blitz? Would he have an 800 number, a web page, or endorsements from celebrities? After a few minutes, share your ideas with the entire group.

▮ ENCOUNTERING THE PARABLES

☐ Choose a different partner and discuss what a mustard seed and leaven have in common. Why did Jesus use household items to talk about the kingdom? Share your answers with the group.

☐ Brainstorm with the group about some of the ways God used tiny beginnings with Jesus, the twelve, the women followers, or Paul's mission team to bring about triumphant outcomes.

☐ With the entire group, explore what the stories of the Sower and the Patient Farmer have to do with the stories of the mustard seed and leaven. God wants to use us to launch his kingdom. How does the wisdom of his approach exceed purely human wisdom? Why is it so effective?

■ BRINGING IT HOME

☐ Allow someone in the group to share a story or two about how God is using small beginnings today in an individual's life, a family's life, or your church. If possible, share some of God's triumphant outcomes.

☐ Ask the group to name some current needs where only God can provide a triumphant end. Where does God's rule need to begin? Where must God intervene? Discuss how the group or individuals might become involved in meeting the need, then pray for God's guidance and intervention.

9

DON'T STAND THERE, DO SOMETHING!

July 4, 1948 is a date that stands out in my memory.

My family had just enjoyed eating a fresh watermelon and my aunt and uncle had just left for their home. After watering the flowerbed on the side of our house, I remember running to the backyard. Suddenly, I fell! The milk bottle, which I had used to water the flowers, had broken and a large piece of glass had cut almost through my left hand. Immediately my parents took me to Vanderbilt University Hospital, where a surgeon in the emergency room cleaned my hand and prepared it for surgery. I still remember him asking me to make a fist with my left hand. I tried as hard as I could, but none of my fingers would move. My hand failed to respond. It was as though a paralysis gripped it. Only after successful surgery could I make a fist.

This is the way life is at times. The very things you want to do, you can't do. And the very things you don't want to do, you do. We want our lives to improve, but somehow we fail to act, failing to respond to what will improve our lives. We become gripped with spiritual and emotional paralysis. Deep feelings of guilt, fear, depression, and loneliness cause us to feel that circumstances control us. Psychiatrist Martin E. P. Seligman describes depression, which is now at epidemic proportions, as "a belief in one's own *helplessness*." He finds in his research that the cloud of depression begins to lift when a person believes that he is not bound by unchangeable circumstances but can take meaningful actions that prove he is not helpless.[1]

Jesus answers our spiritual and emotional paralysis: "Come to me, all you who are weary and burdened, and I will give you rest" (Matt. 11:28). He calls for us to get up, to act, to respond, to open our hearts to him, and to allow him to free us from the circumstances that cause us to feel helpless.

Why does God call for action? Why doesn't he allow us to be simply a meditative or reflective people? Why does God demand something more than an intellectual faith? Why does he use so many injunctions, so many imperatives that call for action in Christianity? Jesus answers these questions in his powerful stories.

Storehouses

Public storehouses were well known in the ancient world. Egypt stored government supplies at the cities of Pithom and Raamses. While in

---

1 Martin E.P. Seligman, "Fall Into Helplessness," *Psychology Today*, June, 1973, 43-48.

Egypt, Joseph laid up a tremendous supply of corn to be used in the years of drought. In ancient Israel, David, Solomon, Jehoshaphat, and Hezekiah all built public storehouses. Such storehouses were quite common in the Mediterranean world.

> The form of one of those ancient granaries is exhibited in a painting of the tomb of Rotei at Beni-Hassan. It consists of a double range of structures resembling ovens built of brick, with an opening at the top of these receptacles, into which the grain, measured and noted, is poured til they are full. The mode of emptying them was to open the shutter in the side.[2]

In addition to these public storehouses, large, private storehouses were also used in the ancient world. They housed corn, or other grain. Private barns were places where threshed corn was stored.[3]

Whether a public storehouse or a private barn, a full storehouse was a sign of prosperity (Deut. 28:8; Prov. 3:10; Luke 2:18) and an empty barn indicated hard times (Joel 1:17).[4]

---

2 John M'Clintock, *Theological and Ecclesiastical Literature*, Vol. 9, (New York: Harper and Brothers, 1891), 1049.

3 Joachim Jeremias, *Rediscovering The Parables* (New York: Charles Scribners Sons, 1966), 130.

4 George A. Buttrick ed., "Barn," *The Interpreter's Dictionary of the Bible*, Vol. 1 (Nashville: Abingdon Press, 1962), 356.

The Wealthy Fool *(Luke 12:16-21)*

It was a family argument. Two brothers were concerned about who would get the most inheritance, property and money. From Jesus' point of view, to immerse one's self in moneymaking and to secure one's life with possessions is to miss the point of living! He illustrates the real point with this story:

I want to tell you about the time a man planted a crop, and the ground produced a tremendous harvest. He began to think to himself, "I've never had such a great harvest. I've had good years before when the rain came just at the right time and when the soil produced bountifully. And I've even had crops that produced a hundred times what I planted. But I have never seen a crop like this one! In fact, I have filled up my warehouse to capacity, and I still have so much left. I'm going to have to think about what to do."

So he thought about it, and he said to himself, "I really don't have many warehouses, and I am going to need a place to put this surplus." He told himself, "I have so much left over that I'll never have to worry again. I've got it made. All I'll need to do now is just sit back and enjoy life. I am secure and have everything I need."

Nevertheless, Jesus warned, "God will come to this man and he will say to this man, 'You are living your life as though I do not exist. You're thinking about all the events of this harvest and all of your life as though I were not around. You're making your plans, deciding on the future, and making all of your decisions totally without depending on me. You know how foolish this is? Tonight, before you get to use any of these things, build the next warehouse, or relax and enjoy all the things that have come to you, I will require of you your life.'"

After finishing his story, Jesus may have turned to those in the crowd and said, "This is how it will be with anyone who stores things up for himself but doesn't rely upon God."

When we secure our lives with "stuff" we've missed the point! Our culture marginalizes God. He is not dead center but peripheral. He's put on the edge of life. But God calls for action because he is primary to life. "Don't just stand there, do something!" God is the only reality that can fill the blank in our lives. There's nothing more significant than relationship with God. A wise person never sees God as negligible or optional. He places God in the absolute core of his life, never at the margins.

God calls for action because he is primary to life.

Stewards

The wealthy of the ancient world placed tremendous confidence in their stewards. A steward was "an official who controlled the affairs of a large household, overseeing the service at the master's table, directing the household servants, and controlling the household expenses on behalf of the master."[5] The Old Testament frequently refers to stewards or estate managers (Gen. 43:19; 44:4; 1 Kings 16:9; Isa. 22:15).

In New Testament times, stewards were not necessarily slaves but sometimes men of esteem. On occasion, a steward would be selected as the treasurer of a city. Paul described Christian leaders as God's stewards in his church (Titus 1:7).[6]

The Unjust Steward (Luke 16:1-8)

Jesus uses the unique relationship between a steward and his master to teach us something important about action.

There once was a man who owned a large estate. He had hired a steward to manage it in his absence. On one occasion the owner checked with his manager to see how well the estate was producing. After talking with the steward, the owner began to wonder about him. He wondered if the steward was a careful man or whether, in fact, he was being too wasteful. Was he embezzling the estate? The

---

5   C.U. Wolf, "Steward, Stewardship," *The Interpreter's Dictionary of the Bible*, Vol. 4, 443.

6   McClintock and Strong, "Steward," *Cyclopaedia of Biblical, Theological and Ecclesiastical Literature*, Vol. 9, 1020.

more the owner of the estate talked with the steward, the more displeased the owner became. He made up his mind to dismiss the steward.

But before such happened, the steward began thinking, "I am going to lose my job. Yet, I'm not strong enough to do harder work; and I've got too much pride to go out and beg." So the steward started thinking about everybody who owed money to the owner of the estate. He went to one debtor and asked, "How much do you owe my master?" And the man said, "Well, I owed him 800 gallons of olive oil." That was a very heavy debt. The steward replied, "I want you to take the bill and write that you owe 400 gallons instead." Next, he went to another man who was indebted to the owner. "What do you owe?", he asked. "I owe him 1,000 bushels of wheat;" replied the second man. The steward told him, "I want you to erase the 1,000 and in its place write 800." Then the steward went back to the owner of the estate and told the owner about these men who owed him some money. But he assured the owner, "I'm on top of this thing. I've got it put together, and they're going to pay you. You're not going to lose it all." And do you know what the owner of the estate said to the manager? He said, "You have done a good job!"

Jesus told his disciples, "The master

commended the dishonest manager because he acted shrewdly. For the people of this world are more shrewd in dealing with their own kind than are the people of the light" (Luke 16:8). So Jesus commended the steward's action to us because we, like the steward, find ourselves in crises that threaten our very existence. Christ calls us to act prudently and responsibly because life is sometimes a pressure cooker. Don't stand there, do something!

Jesus didn't commend the dishonesty of this manager, but commended his resolute, quick action. The crisis did not control the manager. The kingdom of God is composed of people who take resolute, bold, and shrewd actions.

Overseers

In the New Testament times, there were two classes of overseers or stewards. First, there were "guardians"— those entrusted with the care of other people. Second, there were overseers who functioned as managers, administering the responsibilities of the owner. The concept of "delegated responsibility" was at the heart of the function of both classes of stewards.[7]

Steward with Supervision (Luke 12:42-46) and The Talents (Matt. 25:14-30)

To stress the absolute accountability for our

---

7 J.D. Douglas, ed., *The New Bible Dictionary* (Grand Rapids: William B. Eerdmans Publishing Co., 1975), 436-439.

actions, Jesus gives us another story.

A man, who owned a large estate, decided to make a long journey. So he called his steward and placed him in charge of all the other servants. The man failed to tell the steward, though, when he would return. Thus, the steward reasoned to himself, "I'm in charge now. I can do anything I want." He began to beat the other servants, a practice the master had never used. The steward abused his master's trust by holding a lot of drunken feasts and generally ignoring his duties. Then without warning, the master returned in the middle of the night and found the results of his misplaced trust: his possessions had been abused and his servants had been beaten and injured. The master, therefore, punished his steward severely.

Then Jesus concludes, "You must watch and stay ready for the coming of your master."

Again, Jesus stresses responsible behavior in our kingdom business.

There was a certain man of vast wealth who was called away from home for a long period of time. Before he left, he decided that he would entrust his investments to three of his stewards. As a good businessman, he wanted his wealth to reproduce itself. So he called the first steward and gave him five talents—a considerable fortune. Then, he called in the second trusted steward and gave him two talents—still a large amount of money. Next, he called in a third servant and gave him one talent. He gave to each of these servants according to what he thought each could handle, according to their ability. And then he went on his journey.

The first steward, who had five talents, invested those five talents. He took a risk, and it paid handsome dividends-the five doubled to ten talents. The two-talent man looked at his options, took a risk, invested wisely, and also doubled his investment. The one-talent man sat down, looked at his options, and thought to himself: "I could squander it, but I don't want to do that. Or I could sink it in an investment, but that's risky. And I know about my master. He expects profit. I might even lose the one talent I've got. I know what I'll do. I'll dig a hole and hide the talent. That way I won't lose it. And when my master comes back, I'll dig it up and present it to him."

One day the master returned. He called in the man who had been given five talents and was presented with ten talents. The master said, "Well done, servant. You're going to share in my wealth for you have used my wealth responsibly and faithfully."

Then, he called in the second man, who presented him not with two talents but with four. He said, "Well done; you are faithful. You used my investments, and you used them well. You're going to share in my wealth."

Finally, he called in the man who had buried his talent. The steward explained, "I know you don't like to lose money. So you're going to be delighted to know that I didn't lose your money while you were gone. I went out, dug a hole, and hid it. And here it is, just what you gave me before you left." The master dismissed him, saying, "You will not share in my wealth because you are an unfaithful servant. You did not take a risk, nor the opportunity I gave you."

To live in the kingdom is to be given a position of trust. God calls upon us to not abuse his trust. "From everyone who has been given much, much will be demanded; and from the one who has been entrusted with much, much more will be asked," claims Jesus (Luke 12:48b). No need for panic, astrology, or doom. Instead, Jesus calls us to honor the trust God has placed in us.

... Jesus calls for responsible living in the present as the best preparation for the future.

So, what's the point? God expects his people to act. He expects us to use the wealth that he has entrusted to us. I'm not talking so much about money, although he wants us to be responsible stewards of that, too. But his wealth also includes his word, his grace, his mercy, his loving-kindness, and his message. And how about his time? How well do we use it? How well do we use his world? And how about the natural ability that he has given to you and me—our talents and abilities? To squander is to sin. To act shrewdly, wisely, and responsibly is to obey.

God expects us to think, to act cleverly, to be cunning in our stewardship. He expects us to run the risk of failure. He doesn't want us to experience shame or disgrace, but to enjoy the fulfillment of faithfulness. To bury God's wealth, to hide his gifts, is a sin without excuse. He will return, looking for an accounting of his wealth. Jesus calls on us to be like the shrewd steward, and not like the rich fool nor the one-talent man. They are not commended for "sitting steady in the boat." They are condemned because they never saw beyond this world.

An ambitious young man was talking about his life to an elderly, wise man. The young man said, "I will go into business." "And, then?" said the old man. "I will become wealthy," said the young man. "And, then?" said the old man. "I will live comfortably with my family," claimed the young man. "And, then?" replied the wise man. "I shall grow old and retire and live on my money," said the young man. "And, then?" said the shrewd old man. "Well, I suppose some day I'll die." "And, then?"

Questions for Discussion

■ START TALKING

☐ Conduct a brief inventory of the blessings God has given the members of your group. Let each member mention one blessing and move to the next group member until you have circled your group a time or two.

☐ Follow up your inventory with a brief analysis. In what way do our blessings make us feel useful, worthwhile, and accountable? What happens if we don't make good use of our blessings?

ENCOUNTERING THE PARABLES

☐ How can we understand stories about storehouses and stewards when most of us don't own storehouses or employ stewards? How do these stories parallel our lives today?

☐ What's the difference in our attitude toward a gift and a reward? Why is God displeased with an attitude like that of the farmer in Luke 12:16-21?

☐ Is it surprising or troubling when the owner in Jesus' story commends the unjust steward in Luke 16:1-8? Is it astonishing to think that with God's help, we can be clever, shrewd, innovative, and creative?

☐ Is God unfair in these stories? Why does God hold us accountable for the gifts of life, health, family, friends, talents, abilities, opportunities and challenges?

■ BRINGING IT HOME

☐ What are some of the ways we excuse our inactivity? Are there any valid reasons for not being more active? What is the difference between an excuse and a reason?

☐ In what areas of life are you ready to step out in faith and act in the name of Jesus Christ? Will you innovate, think outside the box? Will you devise concrete steps you will take with a family member or friend to encourage, teach, or confront? Build your own list. Ask the group to pray for you now and each step you begin to take.

10

YOU CAN'T LEAP
A CHASM IN TWO JUMPS!

The Battle of the Bulge may be best remembered because of Brig. Gen. Anthony C. McAuliffe. When the Germans demanded his surrender at Bastogne, McAuliffe replied, "Nuts!" But the battle was won by men like Sgt. Charles A. MacGillivary.

A German tank division pinned down his company in the snowy woods near Woelfling, France, on New Year's Day, 1945. MacGillivary had to assume leadership and take action because the Germans had killed the company commander. "As the head of my company, I had a duty to do something," MacGillivary would later say. He set out to personally destroy the German positions, firing two sub-machine guns, hurling grenades, and picking up another machine gun off the battlefield and firing it. He completely wiped out the Germans except for one wounded German who shot MacGillivary with his machine gun. MacGillivary returned his fire and killed the German. Next, in MacGillivary's words, "I looked down and my arm wasn't there." He stuck the stump of his left arm into the snow, which he packed around it till his hand began to freeze. "When they rescued me, my arm had a cake of bloody ice frozen around it, sealing the wound. If it had been summer, I'd be dead." His heroic actions saved the Americans in the woods.

Later, on August 23, 1945, President Harry Truman presented Sgt. MacGillivary with the Medal of Honor. "The guys were freezing to death and my main ambition was to get us out of there," recalled the hero (*The New York Times*, June 30, 2000, C-18).

Charles was a member of what Tom Brokaw eloquently called "The greatest generation any society has ever produced."

> They answered the call to save the world from the two most powerful and ruthless military machines ever assembled. They faced great odds and a late start, but they did not protest. They succeeded on every front. They won the war; they saved the world....A grateful nation made it possible for more of them to attend college than any society had ever educated, anywhere. They gave the world new science, literature, art, industry, and economic strength unparalleled in the long curve of history.[1]

---

1 Tom Brokaw, *The Greatest Generation* (New York: Random House, 1998), xix.

They were committed to their duty, their honor, their country.

Stories of commitment like MacGillivary's are most unusual! We have evolved into a society of off-again, on-again people, vacillating between ardor and apathy. One day our word is our bond; the next day our word is meaningless. One day we're hot; the next day we're not. Is it any wonder that many young people are leery of getting married, teens don't respect their parents, citizens don't trust their government, and church budgets go unmet?

David Lloyd George, Prime Minister of Great Britain, once said, "The most dangerous thing in the world is to attempt to leap a chasm in two jumps." Of course, he's right. You either make it the first time or you don't make it at all! Charles MacGillivary understood that; he jumped!

It's all about commitment. Commitment blends together all we Christians hold dear. It rings up forgotten words like courage, loyalty, honor, duty, passion, and sacrifice: words you don't hear much anymore. But Jesus knew those words. You see, the kind of religion Jesus describes in the parables is not part-time. It is not just lived for one hour on Sunday. You can't clean it up for church and then act differently at work or school. Rather, it is *whole* religion, calling for all of your commitment.

Jesus knows that the only religion worth practicing is one that works in our personal lives—a religion of risk, cost, and commitment.

"I die daily," comments Paul (1 Cor. 15:31). Whatever grips your heart—ambition, wealth, pleasure—wants to rule you. Yet, Jesus wants to rule your heart too! Your heart can't have two rulers. His rule calls for daily death of anything that would rule in his place. He wants to be the Lord of your life as well as the Savior of your soul. "If anyone comes to me and does not hate his father and mother, his wife and children, his brothers and sisters—yes, even his own life—he cannot be my disciple" (Luke 14:26). Hard, tough words! He gives a story to illustrate.

Towers and War

Towers have had a long history in the fortification of cities in the Middle East. A tower might serve several purposes: to defend a city wall, gate, or strategic corner; to observe and attack another city; to serve as a small fortress or alarm post along a strategic area; to protect fields, vineyards, and flocks.[2]

If the work of Herod the Great is an indication of the type of walls and towers built in Palestine, the cost in material and manpower must have been awesome. Even today you can see part of the massive wall, 150 feet high and with stones more than twenty feet in length.[3]

---

2 Merrill C. Tenney, ed., *The Zondervan Pictorial Bible Dictionary* (Grand Rapids: Zondervan Publishing House, 1963), 861; J.D. Douglas, ed., *The New Bible Dictionary* (Grand Rapids: William B. Eerdmans Publishing Co., 1975), 436-439.

3 Ibid., 436-438; Tenney, op. cit., 861.

Ancient armies ranged in size from a small bank of troops to the well-organized legions of the Romans. In the ninth century B.C., Amaziah built an army of 300,000 chosen men of Judah and Benjamin (2 Chron. 25). Throughout the Old Testament, God prepared his people for military conflict. On numerous occasions he had the Israelites send out scouts, who would determine the size, location, and strategy of the enemy. According to the military census taken of Israel at the time of the Exodus (Num. 1), the number of infantry included something over 603,000. By the time of the New Testament, the Romans showed a military genius in their organization, battle strategies, and transportation of troops. Roman military history includes examples of intelligence: scouting out the enemy in order to determine his strengths and capabilities.[4]

Tower Builders and Kings At War
(Luke 14:28-32)

During his early pastoral ministry, Jesus was extremely popular. His healing hand and his comforting message drew followers by the thousands. One day, as large crowds were following Jesus, he spoke to them about one of the key demands of discipleship by using two simple parables.

---

4   Tenney, op. cit., 72-73.

A man decided to build a tower. First, he drew his plans for the tower. Then, he dug down into the earth and began to construct the foundation. He placed large rocks in the ground and built the tower's foundation on them. Soon workmen were busy building it. As people of the city passed by, they could see a tower going up. Then something strange occurred. The carpenters and stonemasons quit coming to the site. Soon the place was vacant. The only thing visible was the foundation. The people of the town began to come by. They told their friends, "I want you to go out with me to see this tower. It's all of a foundation high." And they began to scoff, ridicule, and mock the builder. It seems the builder forgot one thing: he forgot to estimate the cost of building his tower. When he started, he had not thought about the cost in materials and labor to construct his tower.

Then Jesus turned to the multitudes and reminded them that this is why they must count the cost of discipleship. "And anyone who does not carry his cross and follow me cannot be my disciple" (Luke 14:27).

To point out the cost of discipleship in another way, Jesus told a second parable.

A king decided he was powerful enough, had enough troops, and had enough weaponry to defeat his enemy. So he began to mobilize his troops. He trained them and mobilized all of his equipment, but he forgot something. He forgot to estimate the strength of his enemy. He lacked intelligence regarding his enemy's strength. At the last minute he had to make a change. Instead of thinking in terms of war, he had to think in terms of peace. And he had to send a delegation to draw up a peace treaty with his enemy.

Jesus reminded the crowd, many of whom were following him just to get on the bandwagon: "In the same way, any of you who does not give up everything he has cannot be my disciple" (Luke 14:33). Self-testing is crucial to discipleship. Better count the cost before getting on the bandwagon.

Demon Possession

Demon possession frequently occurred in New Testament times. It was not at all uncommon for Jesus and his disciples to meet and deal with demon-possessed persons. Jesus differentiated between those who were emotionally ill and those who were actually possessed by demons. In treatment or therapy of those possessed with demons, he commanded the demon to leave the possessed person (Mark 6:13; Luke 13:32). Demon possession would clearly bring violent and horrible results, such as blindness. It doesn't seem clear just how demons came to live within people. Demon possession continued beyond the ministry of Jesus into the days of the early church (Acts 16:18). Instead of the violence, embarrassment, and horror of having a demon controlling someone, the New Testament offers the option of the Holy Spirit in a person's life.[5]

The Unclean Spirit *(Luke 11:24-26)*

Having just driven an evil spirit from a man, Jesus used the miracle to launch one of his parables.

There was once a man who was possessed of an evil spirit. The demon wreaked havoc through this man's life, turning him into nothing but a house of wickedness and a shattered human being. Finally, this demon left the man and went out into a desert area, where he could hide in the caves. While the demon was out in the wilderness, he found no person in which to live. There was nothing for him to do in the desert, so he decided to return to the man in whom he formerly lived. When he got back to that man's life, however, he found that the man had completely cleaned out his life. Everything was in order and in its proper place. But the demon saw it as an opportunity, not as a rebuke. He went and got seven other evil spirits, and they all came and made their place with him in this man's life.

---

5   For an interesting article on demon possession, see Douglas, op. cit., 1010-1012.

Perhaps, Jesus paused and looked into the eyes of his audience before completing his parable with these words: "And the final condition of that man was worst than the first." Jesus taught that it is not enough for a person simply to subtract the negative—he must also add the positive to his life. Either evil or good rules every person. A religion that only subtracts evil and does not fill up a life with the good is only part Christian. To turn one's life over to Jesus as Lord and allow him to be the new master of one's existence is the essence of Christianity. Jesus calls us to completely commit ourselves to following him as our Savior and our Lord. He

Is not our own personal cross our own personal will and desires that interfere with the will of God for our lives?

wants to be absolutely certain that we do not become counterfeit Christians. "If anyone would come after me, he must deny himself and take up his cross daily and follow me. For whoever wants to save his life will lose it, but whoever loses his life for me will save it" (Luke 9:23-24).

But what is our "cross"? What is it that we must give up if we are to be totally committed to Christ? Is there something we highly value that may stand in the way of our relationship with God? Are we not required, as Abraham was, to give up our "Isaac"? Is not our own personal cross our own personal will and desires that interfere with the will of God for our lives?

If we're going to take up our cross daily and keep counting the cost in our life, what kinds of things must we do? What does it mean to deny ourselves in order to follow Jesus?

Spiritual Changes

Becoming a follower of Jesus Christ is not only a matter of commitment, nor only a matter of subtracting vices from one's life, but also a matter of adding to one's life. At our baptism, we receive "the gift of the Holy Spirit" (Acts 2:38). When God's Spirit begins to give birth to our spirit, changes begin to take place. These changes are spiritual. "The wind blows wherever it pleases. You may hear its sound, but you cannot tell where it comes from or where it is going. So it is with everyone born of the Spirit" (John 3:8). As we sweep what is evil out of our houses, God's Holy Spirit begins to add that which is beautiful and fine. "But the fruit of the Spirit is love, joy, peace, patience, kindness, goodness, faithfulness, gentleness, and self-control" (Gal. 5:22-23a).

Freedom

Jesus insists on careful, deliberate action: no kudos for impulsive, irresponsible action; no place for selfish ambition. It all has to do with freedom. Freedom is not doing exactly as I please without being accountable to anyone—that's phony freedom! Suppose Mrs. Paul Revere had said to Paul, "I don't care who's coming tonight, I have to have the horse!" Well, if she had insisted on doing as she pleased, what would have happened to this country? To recklessly drive a car is not to be free to drive one. Who is free to take pictures? The person who photographs as he pleases? Or the person who is fully accountable to the laws of light, focus, angle, and composition? So, count the cost; determine and plan to accept God's rule, knowing that you're accountable to God. You see, responsible freedom focuses primarily on what it is free for, rather than what it is free from. What we are "free for" is to love God and each other. "You, my brothers, were called to be free. But do not use your freedom to indulge your sinful nature; rather, serve one another in love" (Gal. 5:13).

Jesus reminds us that obedience is the essence of total commitment. But that's a hard saying for us. We are so fiercely independent that we want control of our decisions, money, time, and energies. We're from a culture that stresses individualism and self-made people. We want to "let the record show I did it my way." Surrender to a new master—even Jesus—is not our idea of happiness. So, we encounter the paradox: the only path to genuine freedom and meaning is to not insist on our own rights, privileges, nor our own way. Only when we obey do we experience freedom. No wonder he calls us to jump the chasm!

Questions for Discussion

■ START TALKING

☐ A minister once described the deceased in a funeral eulogy as his foul weather friend. What do you think he meant by that?

☐ Why is it difficult to be a foul weather friend for a large number of people?

■ ENCOUNTERING THE PARABLES

☐ What's surprising about the story of the builder and his incomplete tower? How about the story of the king who made peace?

☐ Reflect on the story of the unclean spirit in Luke 11:24-26. How might it illuminate the concept of full commitment? Which is more important: to fill up our lives with purity, or to get rid of impurities?

☐ Jesus expects any who choose to be his disciples to take their crosses and follow him. Jesus expected some that heard him to make excuses because this commitment costs so much. How does his call to radical commitment sound to modern ears?

☐ Review these three stories and explore the implications each has for the King and his kingdom. Why are these three parables so central in understanding the rule of Jesus in our hearts and lives?

■ BRINGING IT HOME

☐ Many things compete for the central place in our lives. What makes the rule of Jesus Christ in your heart more attractive than anything else?

☐ What most often makes it difficult for you to allow Jesus Christ to rule in your heart? What changes could you make? Is there any way the group might pray and encourage you in your covenant relationship with God's Messiah?

11

CAUTION –
GOD AT WORK!

The story goes this way...

He is remembered for his cunning and able statesmanship at the Congress of Vienna (1814-1815), which was dominated by the four major powers who defeated Napoleon. His name: Charles Maurice de Talleyrand-Perigord. Even though France had caused all the turmoil and should have been severely punished, she got off lightly due to the diplomacy of Talleyrand. Later, a Frenchman asked the astute Talleyrand for his advice on how to start a new religion. "You might want to be crucified and be raised on the third day!" he responded.

When God goes to work, it's awesome! Mysterious! Far-reaching! Beyond our comprehension! No human could have foreseen salvation through a cross! Who would have thought of great work being done in a cemetery? Only God connects the dots of crucifixion and resurrection.

But why was God at work in Christ? After creation, why didn't God simply withdraw? God could have allowed people to go their own way.

Instead, he set about to accomplish something more with his creation. Far from withdrawing, God became deeply and compassionately involved with his lonely, guilty, fearful, and insecure human creatures. Deep within him is the urge to mend broken people.

Caution—God at work!

We now come to a group of parables that concentrate on the nature of God. These parables have two major characteristics. First, Jesus addressed each of these parables to his opponents.[1] He spoke the parable of the two sons to the chief priests and elders of the people (Matt. 21:28). He delivered the parable of the two debtors to Simon the Pharisee (Luke 7:40). And he delivered the parable of the workers in the vineyard to several of the scribes and Pharisees (Matt. 20:1). His main purpose is to defend the gospel against critics who fail to see that God cares about sinners and who are particularly offended by Jesus' practice of eating with the despised.[2]

...God's punctuation mark for history is in the shape of a cross.

Second, each of these parables focuses on a mysterious truth. At the heart of the Christian faith is a strange paradox. If we fail to understand this paradox, we fall into the tragedy of the

---

1   Joachim Jeremias, *Rediscovering the Parables* (New York: Charles Scribner's Sons, 1966), 98.

2   Loc. cit.

Pharisees, chief priests, and scribes. Like them, we fall victim to religious bigotry, prejudice, hatred, legalistic self-righteousness, doctrinal dogmatism, and sectarianism. Here is the paradox: **Love wields more power when it loses than hate wields when it wins.** The best news is the power of self-giving love at the cross of Christ: "But I, when I am lifted up from the earth, will draw all men to myself" (John 12:32).

God's punctuation mark for history is in the shape of a cross. We celebrate the power of self-giving love when we sing, "In the Cross of Christ I Glory, Towering o'er the Wrecks of Time." To a culture caught up in the achievement of immediate results, such a value appears to be sheer insanity. In the deepest understandings of reality, however, we find it true that self-giving love is the greatest power.

Why is self-giving love the greatest power, the best news? Each of the following parables answers this question. Even though it may make no logical sense to human beings, we must remember the sign: "Caution—God At Work!"

Vineyards and Wages

The land and climate of biblical Palestine were almost ideal for vineyards. Rainfall was usually sufficient, and the heat was not too great. Landowners usually planted vineyards on the many hills in Palestine (Isa. 5:1; Jer. 31:5; Amos 9:13). Hired laborers or the landowners themselves usually cultivated the vineyards. But during biblical times it was also a "common practice for a large landowner to rent out his vineyards to a tenant" (Song of Sol. 8:11; Matt. 21:33-43).[3]

The *denarius* was the common silver Roman coin, and it appeared to be the daily wage of a laborer, who worked a full Jewish day (from sunrise to sunset). One *denarius* would equal about sixteen cents. Recall the good Samaritan paid two *denarii* to the innkeeper (Luke 10:35), which suggests something of its purchasing power in the time of Christ.[4]

Workers In The Vineyard (Matt. 20:1-16)

As Jesus moved into Judea, large crowds followed him. Pharisees tested him. The legalistic, self-righteous, religious dogmatists among them misunderstood the activity of God and the rule of God in the lives of people. To them the power of self-giving love seemed like an enigma, a puzzle, a vague threat. To them Jesus said, "Let me tell you a story."

---

3 For background information on vineyards, see J.E Ross, "Vine, Vineyard," *The Interpreter's Dictionary of the Bible*, Vol. 4 (Nashville: Abingdon Press, 1962), 785-786; Steven Barabas, "Vine, Vineyard," *The Zondervan Pictorial Bible Dictionary* (Grand Rapids: Zondervan Publishing House, 1963), 881-882.

4 D.H. Wheaton, "Money," *The New Bible Dictionary* (Grand Rapids: William B. Eerdmans Publishing Co., 1975), 840-841; Alfred Edersheim, *The Life and Times of Jesus the Messiah*, Vol. 2 (Grand Rapids: William B. Eerdmans Publishing Co., 1953), 417.

A man has a vineyard and goes out early one morning to hire people to work in it. He hires several at sunrise and agrees to pay them a denarius, a daily wage. About nine in the morning, he realizes that he has so much work in the vineyard that he needs more workers. So he goes down to the marketplace, where men are standing around talking about the Romans and the weather, and hires them to work in his vineyard. At noon, he realizes there is still a lot of work to be done in the vineyard, so he goes back to the marketplace to hire additional laborers. And again at three in the afternoon, he hires still more. And, then, do you know what the landowner does? At the very last hour of the workday, with only one more hour of sun left in the day, he hires additional workers to labor in his vineyard.

At the end of the day, it comes time to pay the laborers. As he starts to pay the last ones hired, he realizes that they will take home practically nothing to pay for their daily food, clothing, and housing. So he does a great thing! He pays them a full day's wage— a *denarius.* Then, he pays those who had worked all day the same standard wage for a day's labor. But they begin to complain, feeling they have been unjustly treated. The landowner answers each one of them, "Friend, I'm not being unfair to you. Didn't you agree to work for a denarius? As for the men who were hired last, I decided to give

**them the same as I gave you. Don't I have
that right? Could it be that you are envious
because I am generous?"**

Jesus turned to the hard-hearted, stubborn,
dogmatists: "Now do you see," he might have
asked, "why God works the way he does?" Self-
giving love is God's very nature. The single, most
powerful force in the world is the self-giving love
of God, as displayed in Jesus. How easy to think
that people change because of force or threat,
that real power is upward mobility. But God
thinks differently. He works with things like
mangers and moccasins. It's called downward
mobility. It springs from his very nature to love.
Not that we deserve his love. He loves us because
of who he is, not because of who we are. God is
like a landowner who pays his employees, not
according to their merits, but according to his
desire. We can never fully understand God's
grace. God's self-giving love cannot be bound by
our laws, nor by our economics. Who are we to
say how much love God should show to people?

The Two Sons (Matt. 21:28-32)

Why does self-giving love wield such great
power? Why is it that God has opened his rule to
the totally lost—the prostitutes, the poor, the
proud? This is precisely the question of the chief
priests and elders when they asked Jesus, "By
what authority are you doing these things?"
(Matt. 21:23). Their inquiry provided Jesus the

opportunity to tell another story.

One day a man who has two sons tells each of them to go to work in the family vineyard. One son refuses at first to go but later changes his mind and goes. The second son immediately answers, "I will," but he does not go.

"Which of these two sons did the father's will?" asked Jesus. The chief priests and elders answered, "The first son." Then Jesus said to them, "The tax collectors and the prostitutes are entering the kingdom of God ahead of you. For, John the Baptist came to show you the way of righteousness and you did not believe him, but the tax collectors and prostitutes did. And even after you saw this, you did not repent and believe him."

... what power has a religion ... that exalts doctrinal dogmatism and gets nervous about grace... ?

The rule of God is offered to all, Jesus announces. Many lost people eventually accept it. While some religious people appear to do so, they actually refuse it. God's self-giving love wins the hearts and souls of the very people who appear to be far from God. Look how powerful God's self-giving love really is! It changes them from sinners to saints, from persecutors to preachers, from enemies to friends of God. What else can reach sinners who are sick and hurting? What else can offer healing, wholeness, and help?

When self-giving love is offered to sinners, it can bring about repentance and change. *Self-giving love is the greatest power and the best news because nothing else has such power to change people.*

The rule of God is the rule of self-giving love. It meets us where we are, and it changes our hearts. In God's economy, winners become losers and losers become winners. In contrast, what power has a religion that draws the self-righteous and bars sinners, that exalts doctrinal dogmatism and gets nervous about grace, that endlessly repeats its traditions and is silent about self-giving love? Its only effect is to build a wall between its members and God. So, tax collectors and prostitutes enter the kingdom of God ahead of the leaders of such a religion. "Not by might, nor by power, but by my spirit, says the Lord" (Zech. 4:6).

Debt and Debtors

The ancient world dealt severely with debtors, often without regard to their ability or intention to repay. In Athens, before democratic rights were established, a creditor could demand slave labor of his debtor or of members of the debtor's family as surety of payment. Roman law provided punishment by imprisonment to debtors.[5]

The idea of imprisoning a debtor was to

---

5 C. Kathleen Freeman, *The Murder of Herodes and Other Trials From The Athenian Law Courts* (New York: W. W. Norton and Co., Inc., 1946), 14-30.

force him to sell whatever property he might secretly own, have the debtor's relatives pay his debt, or have the debtor and his family work off the debt.

In spite of legal restrictions, the entire system of debts and sureties was recklessly abused in the ancient world. The prophets frequently condemned violations. Ezekiel and Nehemiah called their contemporaries back to a strict observance of the law, where mercy and justice were intended to prevail (Ezek. 18:8, 13, 17; 22:12; Neh. 5:6:13).[6]

Two Debtors (Luke 7:36-50)

Simon the Pharisee invited Jesus to a special dinner, probably in his honor, with other Pharisees. (Since it was considered a meritorious act to invite a synagogue speaker to a meal, some have inferred that Jesus might have just completed a sermon in the local synagogue.)[7] Suddenly, a sinful woman (likely a prostitute) entered the room. Against the custom of the day, she unbound her hair in the presence of the men. Then, she broke the neck of an alabaster jar of perfume and began to anoint Jesus' feet with it. She spread the perfume on Jesus' feet with her hair. It was a shocking scene to Simon and his guests; it provided them with clear-cut proof that

6   G.A. Banois, "Debt, Debtor," *The Interpreter's Dictionary of the Bible*, Vol. 1, 810; A. E. Willingale, "Debt, Debtor," *The New Bible Dictionary*, 304.

7   Jeremias, op. cit., 99.

Jesus was not really who he said he was, or he would not have allowed this sinner to approach and touch him. How could a holy person allow contact with such an unholy person?

Why do you suppose he did allow it? Could it be that her self-giving love was a response of gratitude, rather than one of immoral intent? Was there something in her action that Jesus recognized was missing in the formal politeness of the Pharisees? In answer, Jesus told his fellow dinner guests a story.

Two men owed money to a certain moneylender. The first man owed him 500 *denarii*, and the other owed 50. Neither man had enough money to pay off his debt, so the moneylender canceled the debts of both.

"Which man," Jesus asked, "felt a deeper thankfulness and gratitude?" Simon replied that the one who had the greater debt canceled would feel the deepest gratitude.

Jesus then turned toward the woman and told Simon that her sins had been forgiven—"for she has loved much." In effect, Jesus entreated Simon: "Don't you understand? She's closer to God than you are! She's trying to show her gratitude for the power of self-giving love that God has shown her. But you, Simon, are thankful for very little."

Self-giving love produces gratitude in the life of a forgiven sinner. Jesus apparently had met this woman before and had assured her of her forgiveness by God. Upon seeing him again, she showed her boundless gratitude in the only way she knew how. Her life had been touched by the power of self-giving love. Simon, on the other hand, felt closer to God because he could point to his piety, civic achievement, and moral superiority. The clear lesson of this event is that when we feel a deep gratitude for our personal forgiveness by God, we are closer to God and to his rule than many religious persons who trust in their own abilities, good deeds and piety.

Good News In Strange Circumstances

If hatred, religious prejudice, and bigotry ever looked like winners, it was the day they nailed Jesus to his cross. Here was God's Son, who had never harmed another creature, now abused and mocked. He preached and practiced love, only to be crucified and apparently conquered. But that's only the way it appeared; God went to work and much more happened that day:

> Although he was a son, he learned
> obedience from what he suffered,
> and, once made perfect, he became
> the source of eternal salvation for all
> who obey him and was designated by
> God to be high priest, in the order of
> Melchizedek (Hebrews 5:8-10).

> In him we have redemption through his blood, the forgiveness of sins, in accordance with the riches of God's grace that he lavished on us with all wisdom and understanding (Ephesians 1:7-8).

> But we preach Christ crucified: a stumbling block to Jews and foolishness to Gentiles, but to those whom God has called, both Jews and Greeks, Christ the power of God and the wisdom of God (1 Corinthians 1:23-24).

God's love for people, as shown in the death of his Son, is the best news ever announced. Jesus becomes the only person to live, die, and live again, never to die! All because of the love of God.

Where The Power Is

It is a temptation to feel that the power in Christianity may be found in doctrinal rightness or institutional correctness. We still are tempted to think that we can attract more people if we employ methods other than love. Yet, Jesus said, "But I, when I am lifted up ... will draw all men to myself" (John 12:32). We can be totally

It is a temptation to feel that the power in Christianity may be found in doctrinal rightness or institutional correctness. We still are tempted to think that we can attract more people if we employ methods other than love.

confident that the power at the heart of the
Christian faith is nothing less than the power of
self-giving love. The activity of God at work
among his people is the power of self-giving love.
We are to love those within and those outside the
church. We must tell and show people that we
love them. So, it is important that we not only
agree with the doctrine of love but that we
practice love. That's God's way of working.

Winning Through Defeat

How is God at work on the cross of Jesus?
Consider two insights: (1) hate never looks more
like a loser than when it wins; (2) love never
looks more like a winner than when defeated.

In any given moment, a nail, a scourge, a
bitter cup, or a hammer's blow may appear to
win. A good life breathes its
last breath. Hatred's way of
getting back at people is almost
unbelievable. It can, in the
name of right, produce the

> *Love never looks more like a winner than when it is defeated.*

greatest wrongs. No matter what it looks like it is
doing, hate can only destroy; it has no power to
build. Hate can seduce, but it cannot convince.
Hate can manipulate, but it has no power to
create trust or commitment. That's the scene on
Friday at the cross.

Love, on the other hand, has the power to
endure. Reviled, love does not return the same.
Hurt, it does not retaliate. Bruised and defeated
on a cross, love proves victorious. For, beyond

the moment of death on a cross, it endures as self-giving love—the greatest power ever known on earth. Love rises to endure—never to be defeated. That's the scene on Sunday morning at the tomb. Ernest Freemont Tittle frames it in eloquent language:

> You may place upon the brow of truth a crown of thorns. You may mock truth, scourge it, spit upon it. You may even crucify it between two lies. But ever on the third day it rises from the dead, begins to be seen, heard, and heeded. In any given twenty-four hours love may prove to be no match at all for sheer brute force. A cross-beam, some nails, a hammer, a spear, a sponge dipped in vinegar and lifted to lips in anguish; a loud inarticulate cry as one who has put his trust in love gives up the ghost. But when sheer brute force has had its little day of triumph and vanished from the earth—love is more than ever alive and begins to govern the ages.[8]

---

8 Ernest Freemont Tittle, *Jesus After Nineteen Centuries* (New York: Abingdon Press, 1932), 142-143.

Questions for Discussion

█ START TALKING █

☐ Does our world think of sacrificial love as strength or weakness? Why?

☐ C. S. Lewis admitted that he would have never thought of Christianity, and this had a lot to do with its appeal for him. How many things about the Christian faith could be described as astonishing?

█ ENCOUNTERING THE PARABLES █

☐ Why did Jesus address these parables to his opponents? What common thread ties together the three stories? What might Jesus be trying to tell his opponents about the rule of God? What might his disciples learn by overhearing these stories? What might we learn?

☐ Identify the timeless principles in each of these stories. How does each principle fit our world? Put these stories in words that could fit a scene in your life.

█ BRINGING IT HOME █

☐ How is God's love making a difference in your outlook, relationships, and behaviors? Can you tell of someone in this group or your family who personifies the sacrificial love of Jesus?

☐ Close the discussion with a prayer of thanksgiving for God, the mercy of his son's gospel and the power of the Holy Spirit. Pray for anyone in your group, your family, your neighborhood, or your community who needs to see and hear the love of Christ.

12

BAD NEWS FOR THE ESTABLISHMENT

Police arrested Michael Carter in Connecticut for theft. As they were taking him back to the scene of the crime so witnesses could identify him, he refused to return. "Wouldn't do any good for me to return, I had a mask on!"

We all wear masks. But it's foolish to think you can put a mask on and hide what you really are. How ironic to wear the mask of religion to conceal sins! You know you're wearing a religious mask and hiding your sins when:

- You're content with your understanding of the Bible.

- You're quick to point out sin in other people.

- You rationalize our own personal sin.

- You're quick to point out "how good we are to others."

- You're uncertain about your eternal salvation.

- You study the Bible for information, not transformation.

- You call morally degrading stuff "entertainment."

- You feel spiritually superior to other people.

- You feel no joy in your religious practices.

What God wants us to do is take off the mask. He waits for us to be honest, humble, and to seek his face. If our religion is built around a spiritual superiority complex, Jesus has some bad news for us.

Religious Establishment

At the time Jesus tells his stories, the Jewish religious establishment centers in Jerusalem but reaches out into other parts of the land. The political divisions of Palestine included the territories of Judea, Samaria, Galilee, Perea (eastern side of the Jordan River), northeast Palestine and the Decapolis. There were four institutions in the religious life of first century Palestine: the synagogue, the Temple, the annual feasts, and the Sanhedrin. Of special interest are the six Jewish sects: the Pharisees, the Saducees, the Essenes, the Zealots, the Zadokites, and the Herodians.

The Pharisees were the most prominent sect of the Jews in the first century. All of the evidence points out that no other sect was so influential or numerous. There were probably 6,000 Pharisees, each of whom met certain membership requirements and performed particular pre-scribed religious obligations. The Pharisees were mostly non-priestly scribes and rabbis who were Separatists. This term refers to their emphasis upon ceremonial purity, dietary requirements, and tithing. They were unrivaled in their legalistic observance of the Law. Their loyalty to the traditional exclusiveness of Judiasm "went to the extreme of applying even to members of their own race who were not consistent with their interpretation of the Law."[1] This led to their intense bigotry toward the real sinners of the land—the lower class, outcast, or unclean people.

In addition to their legalistic purity and devotion to the Law, the Pharisees had a profound respect for custom and tradition. They developed a strong confidence in the Jewish oral law, or traditional customs of their religion. By the time of Jesus, their keeping of traditions had built a wall between them and God. That's why Jesus said to them:

> And why do you break the command of God for the sake of your tradition? For God said, "honor your father and mother," and, "anyone who curses his father or mother must be put to

---

1   H.E. Dana, *The New Testament World*, (Nashville: Broadman Press, 1951), 118.

death." But you say that if a man says to his father or this mother, "whatever help you might otherwise have received from me is a gift devoted to God," he is not to "honor his father" with it. Thus you nullify the word of God for the sake of your tradition (Matthew 15:3-6).

The keeping of traditions led them to self-satisfaction. While Jesus did not encourage disobedience to the Law, he showed no regard for a religion based on self-satisfaction.

Another characteristic of the Pharisees was intolerance. They saw themselves as the only loyal ones and demonstrated prejudice toward those different from themselves. They one-sidedly emphasized the external acts of their religion: formal prayers, public fasting, public offerings, and wearing robes with special borders inscribed with scriptures. They worked diligently to convert others to their views. They prided themselves in their noninvolvement with outsiders, especially bad people. Their intolerance and legalism closed their minds to possibilities of change.

Tax collectors are not the objects of great affection in any society, but in the time of Christ, the Jews especially hated them. The Roman government decreed that the taxes of Judea were to be levied by local Jewish collectors who then paid directly to the Roman government.[2] Jews who worked for Rome to collect taxes on their own people were considered traitors. Jewish tax collectors would pay in advance an amount stipulated by Rome for the right to collect taxes in a particular village. Any taxes they could collect above the amount owed to Rome would be profit. Tax collectors had no civil rights, were considered felons, were "disqualified from holding communal office, even from giving testimony in a Jewish court."[3] "Against such unscrupulous oppressors every kind of deception was allowed: goods might be declared to be votive offerings, or a person could pass his slave as his son."[4] So, when Jesus befriended tax collectors, his credibility was questioned by the religious leaders. Because he ate with and touched the unclean, he was accused of breaking kosher laws.

Judiasm prescribes prayer night and day, whenever people need to pray. Formal prayer is made at the same time as Temple services, which is in the morning and in the evening. Three times a day is considered appropriate (Psalm 55:17; Daniel 6:10), with the sixth hour (Acts 10:9) and the ninth hour (Acts 3:1; 10:3, 30) especially

---

2   Alfred Edersheim, *The Life and Times of Jesus The Messiah*, Vol. 1 (Grand Rapids: William B. Eerdmans Publishing Co., 1953), 517.

3   B.J. Bamberger, "Tax Collector," *The Interpreter's Dictionary of the Bible*, Vol. 4, 522.

4   Edersheim, op. cit., Vol. 1, 516.

featured.[5] Temple prayers are usually oral, spoken aloud, and most often sound like reading.[6] A praying person might assume any one of several postures including standing, kneeling, bowing the head, spreading the hands toward heaven, or falling on his face.[7]

Pharisee and Tax Collector (Luke 18:9-14)

For a religious establishment so centered in self-sufficiency and feelings of superiority, Jesus has bad news. It takes the form of a story.

At the appropriate time of daily prayer, two men went up to the temple to pray. One was a Pharisee, and the other was a despised tax collector. The Pharisee chose a prominent place to pray so that others would see him and even hear his prayer. Do you know what the Pharisee prayed? He didn't thank God for God's gifts to him, but he did thank God for one thing—for himself! The Pharisee said, "God, I thank you that I'm not like other men—robbers, evil doers, adulterers—or even like this tax collector." He reminded God of things that he had never done that the tax collector had done. You know what else he prayed? He reminded God of two things that

5   C. W .F. Smith, "Prayer," *The Interpreter's Dictionary of the Bible*, Vol. 3, 866.

6   Joachim Jeremias, *Rediscovering the Parables* (New York: Charles Scribner's Sons, 1966), 111-112.

7   Smith op. cit., 866.

he had done that God hadn't required: he fasted *twice* a week, and he gave a tenth of *all* his income. The prayer was a standard, a formal reminder to God of how devout the Pharisee was.

Then, the tax collector prayed. He chose a less prominent place to pray. In seclusion, he began to pray. Uncomfortable in the presence of a righteous God, the tax collector did not even look toward the direction of God. He felt nothing in himself that would recommend himself to God. So he beat his chest saying, "God have mercy on me, a sinner." The tax collector felt he had done all the wrong things—robbed, committed evil, been unfaithful—and needed forgiveness from a loving God. Both men went home, but only one man went home in a right relationship with God. It was not the Pharisee, who depended upon his own merits of righteousness, but the tax collector, who trusted in God for his righteousness. For everyone who trusts in himself will be humbled, but he who humbles himself and trusts in God will be exalted.

> *It is in trusting, not trying, that God's rule becomes evident.*

To the religious establishment built on self-righteousness, Jesus says that the rule of God cannot enter into their hearts. They don't trust God, they trust themselves. Such self-righteousness is thinly built on comparison to others, self-deception, self-evaluation of one's religious activity, and faulty logic. Humility, on the other hand, offers hope because it is realistic in its evaluation and throws the sinner on God's mercy. Human performance must be swept away. The paradox is that those who trust in themselves, being confident of their right relationship with God, have no relationship with him. Yet, a humble person, who feels he has no relationship with God, is justified by God.

Minas and Tenants

At the time of Jesus, Greek money circulated along with Jewish coins. The basic Greek silver coin was the *drachma*. One hundred *drachmas* equal one *mina*, which is worth about sixteen dollars. One hundred *minae* would be about sixteen hundred dollars—several years' wages in New Testament times.

Those who have studied ancient economics tell us that Jewish law differentiated between commercial interest and increase. In fact, the Old Testament prohibited commercial interest (Exod. 22:25). But by New Testament times, the economy had changed and fair business practices allowed return on commercial investments. Customarily, bankers placed money out at interest rates between four and eight percent.[8]

---

8 Edershieim, op. cit., Vol. 2, 463-464.

The Ten Minas (Luke 19:11-27)
And The Tenants (Luke 20:9-19)

As Jesus approaches Jerusalem, he speaks with directness, even sharpness. The crowds include not only the loyal followers but the curious, the doubters, the impatient, and the stubborn as well. Among those listening to him are members of the religious establishment. To his audience, he stresses the need for faithful service in his kingdom, as well as his own authority as king. Both themes appear in this story:

A man with abilities to rule decided he would go to a country and live among the citizens of that country to become their king. After being invested with the right to rule, he planned to return. Before he left, he called ten of his servants and entrusted each with three months wages—a considerable amount of money. He instructed each to make a capital investment so that when he returned the principal would have gained interest.

Meanwhile, some of his fellow citizens refused to accept his right to rule over their lives; and they objected by saying, "We don't want this man to be our king." He, however, became their king with all the rights and privileges of his position.

Upon returning home, he called in all of his servants so that they might give an account of their investments. The first servant had wisely considered his financial opportunities, had invested, and returned to his king one hundred percent on his original investment. The king rewarded his faithful servant by placing him in charge of ten cities in his kingdom. Likewise, the second servant had invested wisely and returned fifty percent on his original investment. The king placed him over five cities for his faithful service. The third servant, however, failed to use his opportunity to add to his master's original investment, and returned it to him without any increase. The king rebuked him for not using his opportunity and gave the unfaithful servant's original amount to the servant who had been the most diligent.

The king then sent for those who had rebelled at his kingship and had defied his right to rule. He executed extreme judgment toward them.

In this parable, Jesus insists on faithful service in the kingdom; but beyond that, he predicts the downfall of the religious establishment. To those who decide they are the ultimate authority for their own lives and have no need for Jesus as Lord, he undercuts both their rights and their power to do so. He, therefore, exposes their intrigue and opposition to his lordship. This parable proved to be a dangerous one, for it stirred up the anger of the religious establishment.

After telling this parable, Jesus goes on to

Jerusalem. There he clears the temple of religious profiteers and teaches daily in the temple. Yet, the Jewish leaders challenge his authority to do any of this. Their authority challenges God's authority. The clash provides Jesus with an opportunity to tell them a story, a parable of confrontation.

A man planted a vineyard and rented it to some tenants with whom he made an arrangement. At harvest time, they were to take part of the grapes as payment and pay him a share of the harvest. He then went away for a long time on a journey. When the produce from the vineyard began to come in, he sent one of his servants to the tenants to collect his share of the harvest. But the unprincipled tenants decided to take advantage of the owner, who lived at a distance. So they beat the servant and sent him away with none of the harvest.

The owner sent another servant, whom the tenants beat and treated shamefully. The owner then sent a third servant, and they paid him with injuries and threw him out.

The owner decided that such severe actions on the part of his tenants deserved the most extreme response. He decided to solve the problem by sending his beloved son to the tenants. He thought they would respect him. But the rebellion of the tenants was so great that they decided to kill the son so the vineyard might be theirs. So the son suffered and died.

"What then will the owner of the vineyard do to them?" asks Jesus. "He will execute judgment on those tenants and give the vineyard to other people."

Here Jesus draws a symbolic picture of Israel's long religious history. He reminds the Jews of Isaiah's picture of Israel as the vineyard of God (Isa. 5:1-7). God repeatedly extends his long-suffering toward them by sending his prophets, his messengers, and even John the Baptist. But the religious establishment refuses his messengers. The breakdown of the relationship between Israel and God is near. No wonder, then, that when Jesus approaches Jerusalem and sees the city, he weeps over it (Luke 19:41).

To Forgive or Not To Forgive
(Matthew 18:21-35)

As Jesus surveys the religious establishment of his day, he notices a fundamental flaw in their practice of religion. While they talk about mercy, they fail to practice it. So he decides to tell them a story.

Once a king wanted to settle accounts with all of his servants. One of them owed him several million dollars. Since the man was unable to pay such an enormous debt, the king ordered that he and his family should all be sold to repay the debt. The servant began to plead, "Be patient with me and I will pay

you back everything." Guess what the king did? He cancelled the debt and let him go.

Not long afterward, that same man went out to one of his fellow servants who owed him a few dollars. He grabbed him by the throat and threatened him, "Pay back what you owe me." His fellow servant begged him from his knees, "Please be patient with me and I will pay you back." But he refused and threw the man in jail until he could pay his debt. Later, the king heard what had happened and called in his servant: "You're a wicked man. I cancelled all your debt at your request. Why didn't you show mercy to your fellow servant, just as I did to you?" In anger, the king threw the man into jail until he could pay back all he owed.

To a religious establishment that doesn't know the power of forgiveness, Jesus drives his point home: "This is how my heavenly father will treat each of you unless you forgive your brother from your heart." But it's too much for a self-righteous religious establishment to bear!

Bad News/Good News

Why does Jesus have such bad news for the religious establishment? What is it that he knows that the religious establishment has not learned?

Jesus knows that God's presence comes only when God's people humble themselves. "Seek the Lord, all ye humble of the land ... seek humility" (Zeph. 2:3). Every time people humble themselves, God responds with his presence. When Josiah "tore his robes," God was there (2 Kings 22:19). When Manasseh "humbled himself greatly," God forgave him (2 Chronicles 33:12). God is not moved by men of standing, but by men of kneeling.

Why is there not more revival in today's churches? Why are so many churches dead? The answer may shock us: how can we expect God to come and live in our hearts if we have not repented, gone to our knees in humility, or fasted to show our humility before God? If we feel no burden for our sins, if we fail to be broken, if we're satisfied with the state of our churches, then we may look more like the religious establishment of Jesus' day than we really intend.

If we feel no burden for our sins, if we fail to be broken, if we're satisfied with the state of our churches, then we may look more like the religious establishment of Jesus' day than we really intend.

Why does Jesus have such wonderful news for the repentant? He knows that the repentant person feels great gratitude for forgiveness. Jesus knows that when a person turns to God with a burdened heart he becomes aware of how far removed he really is from God. A new beginning is near. The irony of it all is that Christ comes and the "unprepared" accept him, while the "prepared" reject him. So, the Pharisee stumbles home under the burden of self-satisfaction while the tax collector runs home, free from his guilt.

Today, the church still hears the stories of Jesus. It is easier to draw lines, eliminate sinners and have respectable churches. It's always risky to reclaim the lost. But Jesus is not looking for respectable churches. He's looking for repentant churches.

Remember: God will consent to live only with the broken and humble. Whether we're talking about hearts or churches ... the proud need not apply!

Questions for Discussion

◼ START TALKING

☐ If a new person joined this group today, why might he or she feel like an outsider?

☐ Would your group be eager to make a visitor a part of the gang? Why do some groups draw boundaries that make others feel excluded?

◼ ENCOUNTERING THE PARABLES

☐ Why were tax collectors of Jesus' time considered outsiders? Why was the Pharisee an insider? What might have surprised Jesus' listeners about the outcome of this story?

☐ Think of those listening as Jesus told the story of the minas and the tenants. How do you think the Pharisees and teachers of the law might have reacted? Jesus' disciples? The wealthy landowners in the crowd? A blind beggar? Which reaction would most resemble yours as you heard the story?

☐ In the forgiveness story in Matthew 18:21-35, what is the bad news in this story for the religious establishment? Is it surprising that the religious leaders would fail to be people of forgiveness?

☐ React to the statement, "Jesus is not looking for respectable churches, but repentant churches." Can you think of religious persons who might be shocked or offended by this idea?

■ BRINGING IT HOME

☐ What masks do you wear at church? At home? At work? How might these masks keep your heart from being humbled and broken? Is there anyone whom you trust enough to let them see your brokenness?

☐ Share your brokenness with a group committed to strict confidence. Close with prayer for healing from God and the help of his Holy Spirit. Make a covenant with a few trusted people to experience regular times of confession and prayer.

13

WHEN THE IMPOSSIBLE HAPPENS

Jim Collins shatters myths—especially myths about successful organizations. Myths like, "Great companies are led by great leaders." Or, "Highly successful companies make their best moves by brilliant planning." Jim's quiet demeanor and youthful appearance belie the fact that he won the Distinguished Teaching Award at Stanford University's Graduate School of Business.

He spent six years studying visionary companies and published his results in *Built to Last*. He found that such companies don't always have visionary leaders nor are they especially great places to work. Rather, they almost never change their core values and they make bold commitments to "Big Hairy Audacious Goals." Their goals may be risky and wild, but the challenge captures the hearts of people, gets their juices flowing, and builds enormous momentum. While his research focused on businesses, he challenged several of us in ministry to "build an enduring church" while at a Colorado Springs Leadership Conference Retreat. His question to us: "What per cent of churches represented in this retreat will be stronger in thirty years?" Our answer: less than twenty per cent!

A number of years ago, the head of DuPont's research division called together all of those who had worked at making and producing film. "Forget what you know about film," he told his audience of distinguished research scientists, "and see a vision of what can be done with film." Given such a challenge, DuPont scientists began working on a new film—the strongest film ever developed. They developed a film strong enough not only to make a movie, but to pull a car.

"Church." What comes to your mind? For a moment, forget what you know about church and see a vision of it could be. Dream of what a church could accomplish, could achieve. Careful about the myths! Think outside the box. See people served, worship offered, needs met, changes made, sins confessed, lives transformed. Routine, ritual, cynicism, and decline may have jaded our ability to dream the impossible dream. Maybe we need to recapture and restore the dream of what the church really can be. Maybe we need to believe the impossible can happen! Jesus did! He not only believed the dream, he died for it!

In his parables, Jesus gave us a momentary glimpse of enduring Christianity as the dream of God. God sees his kingdom as "built to last." His stories show that God works way outside the box. He thinks of the impossible as normal. He looks way beyond what we see. He views moments from an eternal perspective. Most will miss it. It's up to us—each of us. "He who has ears, let him hear," Jesus warned (Matt. 13:9).

Before turning to two more of Jesus' stories, it is helpful to understand that the meaning of these parables was not always clear to those who heard them. Jesus explained that "the knowledge of the secrets of the kingdom of heaven has been given to you, but not to them" (Matt. 13:11). Then, he unveiled for us the operational principle by which God allows men to understand the principles of kingdom life: Whoever acts on the truth he has will receive more; whoever does not act will lose the truth he has (Matt. 13:12).

Weeds

"Tares" were an annual poisonous rye grass that was very common in the Middle East. Commonly found in wheat fields, it looked almost exactly like wheat until the ear appeared. The roots of tares would creep underground and become intertwined with those of the wheat. Consequently, if the tares were pulled up, so was the wheat. Because tares were noxious, the wheat had to be separated from it at harvest. After harvest, the wheat was fanned and then put through a sieve. The smaller rye grass seeds left after fanning passed through the sieve, leaving the wheat behind.[1] In some instances, women

---

1   John L. Leedy, "Plants of the Bible: Tares," *The Zondervan Pictorial Bible Dictionary* (Grand Rapids: Zondervan Publishing House, 1963), 668.

and children were given the tedious, manual task of separating the wheat from the tares.[2] The tares were bound into bundles and burned—not as waste but as fuel.[3]

The Weeds And The Wheat
(Matt. 13:24-30; 36-43)

One day as Jesus sat by the Sea of Galilee, large crowds gathered to hear him speak about kingdom life. Even though he knew that some of his hearers would not understand, he knew, nevertheless, that some in his audience would catch on. Rabbis work that way.

A man plowed his soil and prepared his field for sowing. He then sowed good wheat seed in his prepared field. But one night the man's enemy came and sowed weeds among the wheat. Of course, there was no way to tell that the wheat and the weeds were not the same until the blades appeared.

The owner's servants came to him and said, "Where did the weeds come from? Didn't we sow good wheat seed in the field?" The owner replied, "My enemy did this, perhaps for revenge."

The servants then asked the owner of the wheat field, "Do you want us to go and pull

---

2 J.D. Douglas, ed., "Tares," *The New Bible Dictionary* (Grand Rapids: William B. Eerdmans Publishing Co., 1975), 1238.

3 Joachim Jeremias, *Rediscovering The Parables* (New York: Charles Scribner's Sons, 1966), 177.

up the weeds?" "No," he answered, "because damage will result to the wheat by premature separation. Let them both grow together until the harvest. And at that time I'll tell the harvesters to first collect the weeds and tie them in bundles to be burned, and then to gather the wheat and bring it into my barns."

When Jesus finished the parable, the crowd left. Then his disciples said to him, "Explain to us the parable of the weeds in the field." And he answered:

> The one who sowed the good seed is the Son of Man. The field is the world, and the good seed stands for the sons of the kingdom. The weeds are the sons of the evil one, and the enemy who sows them is the devil. The harvest is the end of the age, and the harvesters are angels. As the weeds are pulled up and burned in the fire, so it will be at the end of the age. The Son of Man will send out his angels, and they will weed out of his kingdom everything that causes sin and all who do evil. They will throw them into the fiery furnace, where there will be the righteous will shine like the sun in the kingdom of their Father. He who has ears, let him hear (Matthew 13:37-43).

Seine Nets and Fishes

Fishing was not only very lucrative, but it also provided a favorite food on the table of many a Jewish family. Even Caesar enjoyed fish from Galilee. Today, "St. Peter's fish" from the Sea of Galilee is served as a delicacy on tables throughout the Middle East. So important was the ancient fishing industry that one of the gates in Jerusalem was called the Fish Gate.[4]

The New Testament describes several scenes of fishermen washing, mending, or casting their nets. The seine net is a special kind of dragnet by which several fishermen cover a bed of fish with the net and then drag it to shore. The seine net "is either dragged between two boats or laid out by a single boat and pulled to the land with long ropes."[5] When the seine net is pulled to shore, fishermen begin to separate the clean fish from the unclean fish. According to Leviticus 11:9-12 and Deuteronomy 14:9-10, clean fish were those having scales and fins, while unclean fish were those without fins and scales, such as shell fish.[6]

The Seine Net *(Matt. 13:47-52)*

In order to unveil the secrets of kingdom life, Jesus told the story of the seine net. It's a

---

4   Alfred Edersheim, *The Life and Times of Jesus The Messiah*, Vol. 1 (Grand Rapids: William B. Eerdmans Publishing Co., 1953), 473.

5   Jeremias, op. cit., 177.

6   J.A. Thompson, "Fish, Fishing," *The New Bible Dictionary*, 424.

simple, brief story with universal, future implications.

One day a large number of fishermen took their dragnet and let it down into the lake. They began to drag it through the waters of the lake toward the shoreline. When the dragnet was full, the fishermen pulled it upon the shore. Then, they sat down and began to collect the clean fish into baskets. But they threw the unclean fish away.

Jesus then turned to his disciples and told them, "This is how it will be at the end of the age. The angels will come and separate the wicked from the righteous and throw them into the fiery furnace, where there will be weeping and gnashing of teeth" (Matt. 13:49-50). Imagine their faces, their expressions!

The Impossible Way

Here's the way God's rule works: it grows slowly and gradually, like all other living things, by organic development. In the story of the weeds, Jesus tells us "... the good seed stands for the sons of the kingdom" (Matt. 13:38). If we open our hearts to God's rule, God plants us in the world. No fruit yet, just a plant. That anything very significant could happen seems impossible. But God works by his own time frame. He knows growth requires patience and perseverance. It's his agenda, his program of

Christ in the hearts of people.

It's like the story of Amy, who once entertained men as an exotic dancer. Night after night she danced at "gentlemen's clubs," making over $500 per evening. Soon she landed a job as the featured dancer, making a base salary of $1,000-$3,000 a week, plus tips and expenses. Offers from porn magazines and movies began to pour in. Her goal: a featured layout in *Playboy* magazine.

Yet, Amy was paying a dear price. "My success gave me a false sense of self-esteem. While

Growth takes place when a faithful life reproduces itself.

on stage I felt famous, but there was still a void in my life. I remember asking God to help me out so many times before, I was scared to ask him again." After a tremendous spiritual struggle, Amy turned to God: she walked out for the last time. "It was light outside when I walked away. I knew I would never go back to that darkness again."

Today, as faithful followers of Christ, Amy and her husband have started "Amy's Friends." Located in Dallas, it is a support group to help women make the transition out of the sexual entertainment business. Highly successful, "Amy's Friends" is giving hope, faith and direction to lives that were headed for disaster. God has planted Amy in the world so she can yield a great harvest for him. She says, "I thank God every day for this second chance."

Interesting how people have continually misread God's movement. Since the time of

Jesus, some have expected the kingdom to come with dramatic catastrophe, not by gradual growth. Apparently, so many at Thessalonica thought the second coming was near that they quit work. Since then, others have again and again predicted the second coming of Jesus. Even as we moved into the new millennium, 40% of U.S. adults believed the world would end and 36 million Americans believed the end times would come during their lifetimes (*Newsweek*, Nov.1, 1999). Not only have all of these predictions about the date of the second coming been wrong, they've missed a fundamental truth of God's rule. God grows his kingdom like he grows other living things—by organic development, not by catastrophe. Catastrophe or sudden, dramatic, momentous actions may make the evening news, but it's not the way God usually works. Spiritual growth takes place when a faithful life reproduces itself. In fact, the biological test for growth is whether or not an organism can reproduce itself. God looks for faithful workers in the kingdom who can reproduce his rule in other receptive, open lives.

Growth lasts from seed time to harvest time. God's rule takes root in the life of an open, sincere heart. Like a gardener, he plants his truth in the world. The seed is powerful. The influence, character, and actions of a faithful disciple work into the receptive lives of others. Growth is slow! It's gradual! It develops like all other living things—by organic development.

Leave The Gardening To God

Another principle of kingdom life surfaced in the story of the weeds: attempts to purify the kingdom must be left to God, the Gardener. In

God is the gardener, not man nor any group of men.

the parable of the weeds, the servant asked the master, "Do you want us to go and pull the weeds up?" "No," the master answered, "because while you are pulling the weeds, you may root up the wheat with them. Let both grow together until the harvest ..." (Matt. 13:28-30). Without question, the work of Satan intrudes into the work of the kingdom. He uses several strategies designed to slow or kill the growth of God's kingdom:

- Deadly sins
- Apathy
- Division
- Malicious evil
- A fault-finding spirit
- A spiritual inferiority complex

No doubt, Satan has planted his own people in God's field. But notice this: human efforts to purify the church always fail! From the Donatists (4th century A.D.)—who tried to purify the church of heresy—to modern zealots, damage is always done to the church. God never commends irresponsible zeal. Neither does God commend impatience. God never commends those who try to take over his place. He has no compliments for those who try to appear holier than he is. God is the gardener, not man nor any group of men. We must allow God to be God; he will purify his own kingdom in his own time and in his own way: "The Son of Man will send out his angels, and they will weed out of his kingdom everything that causes sin and all who do evil" (Matt. 13:41).

Faithful In Heart

The parables of the weeds and the seine net point us to another fundamental principle of kingdom-life: it is the task of the people of God to be faithful in heart. When the Bible uses the word "heart," it does not refer to the muscle that pumps blood to the body. Instead, the "heart of man" is the very center of man's inner life and the source of his will power. "The heart is supremely the one centre in man to which God turns, in which the religious life is rooted, which determines moral conduct."[7] The heart is the place in man where God's Spirit convinces man's spirit that God should rule man. My friend Anton Farah of Nazareth says that in Judaism, you hear with your heart, listen with your ear, and understand with your mind. "For it is with your heart that you believe and are justified..." (Rom. 10:10). Jesus says that the message about the kingdom is "sown in a person's heart" (Matt. 13:19).

---

7   Behm, "Kardia," *Theological Dictionary of the New Testament*, Vol. 3 (Grand Rapids: William B. Eerdmans Publishing Co., 1965), 612.

The difference between the wheat and the weeds or the clean fish and the unclean fish is a difference in heart. For, when God's rule takes root in a receptive, contrite, open, and broken heart, the process of salvation begins. It reaches its climax at harvest time. With Jesus, the issue is never in doubt! Harvest time is inherent in the seed. Christ breaks through and into a person's life by coming into her heart. The task of that person's life is to be faithful in heart.

What is the future of the kingdom of God? Think for a few minutes of what the church can be. Do everything within your own power to see that the kingdom is a victorious reality in the lives of people.

Questions for Discussion

■ START TALKING

☐ Think of the world's oldest civilizations. How long did they last? How many businesses or corporations can you name that have been in operation for more than a century? What do human organizations have in common with human beings?

☐ Even Christian congregations often seem to have a seasonal life cycle. What is your evidence for believing that God's kingdom is eternal? Explain your answer.

ENCOUNTERING THE PARABLES

☐ Jesus clearly explained to his listeners what was symbolized in this parable by the weeds and the wheat. Did anything in his explanation surprise you? How does Jesus' attitude toward impurities in the field contrast with what you might have expected? What are the implications for our congregations? For our relationships?

☐ Discuss your reaction to the phrase "secrets of kingdom life." What aspects of life in Christ's kingdom are presently hidden from us? When will these secrets be revealed?

☐ In the seine net story, what new and astonishing things do we learn about the nature of the kingdom?

☐ What is the difference between the organic development of a person's life and a sudden catastrophe? Why is time necessary for Christian growth after planting a seed? In the parable of the wheat and the tares, God is presented as the farmer, the one responsible for the condition of the wheat field. What are the implications for the church?

BRINGING IT HOME

☐ What sort of spiritual growth takes place when a faithful life reproduces itself? What are your goals and aims in reproducing your faith?

☐ Putting together your group experiences of the last thirteen weeks, set some goals for implementing the lessons of these stories. Share one or two of your goals with the group. Close with a special prayer that God will help your group make the impossible happen.